THE
CRYSTAL
BUCKET

THE
CRYSTAL
BUCKET

*Television criticism from
the Observer 1976-79*

Clive James

JONATHAN CAPE
THIRTY BEDFORD SQUARE LONDON

First published 1981
Text copyright © 1976, 1977, 1978, 1979 by the Observer
Introduction copyright © 1981 by Clive James

Jonathan Cape Ltd, 30 Bedford Square, London WC1

British Library Cataloguing in Publication Data

James, Clive
The crystal bucket.
1. Television programs – Great Britain – Reviews
I. Title
791.45'0941   PN1992.3.G7
ISBN 0-224-01890-6

Set by
Gloucester Typesetting Co. Ltd
Printed in Great Britain by
Lowe & Brydone Printers Limited, Thetford, Norfolk

to Peter Porter

And by the happie blisfull way
More peacefull Pilgrims I shall see,
That haue shooke off their gownes of clay,
And goe appareld fresh like mee.
Ile bring them first
To slake their thirst,
And then to taste those Nectar suckets
At the cleare wells
Where sweetnes dwells,
Drawne up by Saints in Christall buckets.

Sir Walter Ralegh,
The passionate mans Pilgrimage

Contents

Introduction

This book continues the story which I started to tell in *Visions Before Midnight*, a volume selected from my *Observer* television column between the years 1972 and 1976. In this second instalment I try to cover the years 1976–1979, but once again the story is patchy. There is no hope of telling it all, or even of outlining all the reasons why this should be so. Enough to say that British television remains too various to be fully absorbed by one mind, even when that mind is well accustomed to being bombarded by patterns of light and sound for the better part of every day. All politico-sociological or sociologico-political surveys of British television can safely be dismissed as moonshine. In America there might be some chance of summing up what the networks crank out, but in Britain your only chance to draw fully abreast of what the BBC has on offer is when ITV goes on strike, and vice versa. Far from being a conspiracy to manipulate the public, British television is an expanding labyrinth which Daedalus has long since forgotten he ever designed.

Most of the blandness which experts presume to detect in television is really just the thinness of overtaxed inspiration, as programme-makers desperately try to come up with something original once or thirteen times too often. The production of television programmes is governed by considerations which have little to do with any supposed calculation of the effect on the punters. It is a mark of how times have changed that I can advance this proposition without sounding even mildly paradoxical. Only ten years ago it was regarded as unquestionable that the basic attitude of television executives was cynicism. ('Basic' was as basic a word then as 'situation' is now.) With regard to the ITV companies the cynicism was presumed to be commercially determined. With regard to the BBC the Establishment was presumed to be manipulating the collective mind of the working class in the interests of a reactionary consensus. You couldn't switch on a television set without being brought face to face with some humourless pundit telling you how television was a repressive mechanism.

Talk of decades is essentially trivial but triviality has its place. Many people were thrilled by the 1960s and disappointed by the 1970s. For wiser heads, however, it was the other way around. The 1960s were a binge and the 1970s were the hangover. But unlike a real hangover it had no element of remorse. The headache was barely half dissipated before everybody had forgotten just how ridiculous his or her behaviour had previously been. Forgetfulness is not good but it is better than thoughtlessness, especially when the thoughtlessness is dignified with the name of ideology. The 1960 radical critique of the Capitalist Media had scarcely a thought in its head. Whether teaching in Cambridge or contributing to *Time Out*, people who could barely compose a readable sentence laid down the law about how television was part of a vast conspiracy to stifle the inventiveness of the people. Inspiration, it was assumed, lay thick on the ground, waiting to be picked up. Enlightenment was in the air. Would the television organisations respond to this challenge, or would they have to be dismantled? Something called the Free Communications Group proposed the breaking up of the BBC – a move guaranteed, it was confidently asserted, to increase freedom, especially in communications.

Such was the intensity of 1960s euphoria that people whose biggest achievement had been to write some shoestring polemical article felt as creative as the Beatles. In the 1970s most of these no longer young hopefuls graduated into a fretful quiescence. The best of them achieved a kind of tentative ceased to be unforthcoming is in the question of Northern Ireland. My own view is that both organisations would do better to let the documentary-makers have their heads on this subject, but I can see how to an executive it might seem otherwise. Each channel has provided a complete historical analysis of the Ulster situation (for once the word is appropriate) at least once. They could do that every week and not change matters. Nor would they necessarily change anybody's mind. Television, I suspect, can do little in the short term to ameliorate a political crisis, although there can be no doubt that it can do much to exacerbate it. But leaving that vexed point aside, it is still notable that in the area of political journalism ITV has been at least as active as the BBC.

Beyond the IBA's relatively modest requirements on the holders of a franchise, there is no reason why the ITV companies should do as much as they do to appear serious. They do so, it seems to me, for honour's sake, and because even in the counting house there are many mansions. The ITV companies have undoubtedly done more than their share to promote mind-rot among the populace. Their imported game-show formats give an unnervingly pungent whiff of what American television is like from daylight to dusk. But there the resemblance stops. Not even the less discriminating of the commercial companies are entirely without pride. It is not always just their money that attracts restless BBC personnel, it is often the opportunity they provide to do something original. While this book was in production, Dennis Potter and several other subversive talents were engaged in making programmes for a commercial television company, LWT. But the trail was already blazed. It was ITV, not the BBC, which made and screened *Bill Brand*, a decidedly radical series in which the hot-eyed hero poured scorn over piecemeal solutions and resolutely refused to be tamed. *The Naked Civil Servant*, Jack Gold's brilliant programme about Quentin Crisp, was turned down by the BBC and triumphed as an ITV offering. Neither of these ventures could be seriously thought of as demonstrating even the slightest trace of commercial cynicism. The worst you could say was that ITV had begun to usurp the BBC's function. As if to endorse this analysis, BBC executives started showing a strange inclination to cancel potentially awkward programmes after they had actually been made, or – as in the case of *Law And Order* – to fight shy of them after they had been screened. But that was a question of personality. It had little to do with the analyst's favourite word, structure.

British television is simply not to be compared with the American networks, of which the film *Network* gave such a precisely inverted picture. On American television little untoward is allowed to happen. On British television the untoward happens all the time. It is a matter of how things are organised. Even the most money-minded of the ITV companies can't function without programme-makers, and the programme-makers have been brought up in a tradition of pride in work. This is just the kind of tradition which radical criticism is least equipped to understand. It is, if you like, part of the superstructure.

Inevitably the schedules eke out their surprisingly high proportion of good things with an even higher proportion of junk. Even then, such is the pressure of continuous programming that much of the junk has to be imported. Not all of these interloping programmes are entirely to be despised. A general opinion about American private eye series, for example, is not worth hearing if it does not leave room to remark that *The Rockford Files* is consistently engaging and often very sharply written. Even *Charlie's Angels* has some sort of virtue, if only as an indication of the true depth to which feminism has penetrated the American networks. After the Angels had completed their first series an Oxford English don wrote an article declaring that they were the only thing worth watching on television, whose serious programmes were beneath the contempt of such demanding intellects as himself, but whose lapses into abject trash might accidentally stimulate his creative imagination. In his case the Angels certainly seem to have done the trick. Next time I saw him in the flesh he was wearing an ear-ring. Perhaps *Dallas* will do the same for me. I came to mock *Dallas* but I stayed to pray. In how many directions could Sue Ellen move her mouth? Which of the four leading ladies would be wearing the bra this week? Would Jock's love for Miss Ellie survive her mastectomy? Perhaps Miss Ellie's missing breast would be invited to star in a series of its own – a spin-off.

Sometimes the imported product was better than ours, especially in the field of documentary drama. From *The Missiles of October* down through *Washington Behind Closed Doors* to the magnificently acted *Blind Ambition*, the Americans showed us how to make television drama out of domestic politics. The British companies could work something like the same trick when the subject was royalty – *Edward and Mrs Simpson* was the outstanding achievement in that line, if you don't mind the almost total distortion of the leading characters – but when it came to Downing Street coyness supervened. The fact of closed government leads to conjectural fiction. In America, where everything is out in the open, the framework of a screenplay is already there in the congressional record. The naive candour of open government survives into the fictional treatment, giving it the freshness of an adventure story.

That same naivety carried all the way through to *Holocaust*, which I did not find at all contemptible, despite being told to by a chorus of knowing voices. It is wishful thinking to suppose that an historical memory can be transmitted without being simplified. The memory is already simplified before people decide that it needs to be transmitted. All you can hope for, in this most extreme of all cases, is for a sense of outraged decency to be embodied in a way that will touch the feelings of the uninformed. People who thought they knew a lot about the death camps might have been unmoved by *Holocaust*, but people who knew little were often moved to tears. To scorn the series was easy. The Jews looked more Aryan than the Nazis. But calling the series a melodrama could not cancel the fact that there was real drama mixed into it. What more could you ask in the portrayal of helpless anguish, how much more could the heart take, than Meryl Streep provided in her role as the wife driven to distraction by the sight of her tortured husband? The budget would have had to be a lot lower, the minor roles much more caricatured than they were, before such a performance lost its emotional impact. Meryl Streep is a greatly gifted artist who will spend her life doing famous things, but I doubt that she will ever do anything more important.

Yet even by saying that much I can hear myself trying to make you remember, whereas life would be choked by thought if we did not forget. Most television is bound for oblivion and rightly so. In ways that blessedly cannot be quantified, the programmes to which gifted people have devoted months and sometimes years of their lives make fleeting marks behind our eyes and slip away. Nobody can be sure about what television does to the viewer. One opinion holds that television programmes can subjugate whole populations and turn children into murderers. Another opinion holds that television is too trivial a cultural event to be considered. A surprising number of experts have subscribed to both these opinions in close succession or even simultaneously. I never cease to be stunned at the assurance with which moralists pronounce about the precise manner in which large numbers of people are affected by sounds and images transmitted invisibly through space. I have enough trouble answering for myself.

In a given year of viewing I am regaled with as much dramatic fiction as Aristotle faced up to in a lifetime; more great music than the most passionate nineteenth-century music lover would have heard if he had lived to be a hundred; more facts and figures than I care, or dare, to think of. The head would come off its hinges if it were asked to remember what happened last year as well. So the mind protects itself, with the coarse filter of forgetting. The insubstantial pageant fades. We hope it leaves a wrack behind, but can't be sure what the wrack is. As we wait for introspection to provide the answer, the parade inexorably continues, like the triumphal march from *Aida*, like the Panathenaean procession, like those interminable allegorical displays in the Middle Ages. Why should so many talented people put so much effort into what will be forgotten? And most of it *will* be forgotten, no matter how dedicated the efforts to preserve it. The frightful blunder by which the BBC wiped the tapes of plays by Pinter, Owen, Gray and other leading playwrights was merely a prematurely terminal instance of what would have happened anyway in the course of time. I like the idea of a channel for important repeats but residual payments would make it difficult to organise. And if a channel won't organise it then the individual viewer is unlikely to either, even if all the past material were available from an instantaneous and inexpensive form of data-retrieval. There is barely time to view the present. To view the past as well would take all the time in the world. So ephemerality is likely to go on being the condition of life for everyone who works in television.

But it never seems that way at the time. Whether as a viewer or as a participant, I have never been able to feel above the battle. Unfortunately MacNeice's lines in 'The Sunlight on the Garden' come truer every day. *Our freedom as free-lances/Advances towards its end.* Year by year it gets harder to be a solo act. The fourth channel and the new technology might combine to safeguard the future of the independent contributor but I'm not counting on it. Soon work will be rationed, nobody will be allowed to have two jobs, and anyone who wants to appear on television will have to sign on with a company.

On that day there will be a clear conflict of interests and I will be through as a television critic. But I hope I am left with the choice. A project I once put up to a television company was turned down on the grounds that I had not yet decided which side I was on. I believe that there is only one side and no war. There is just television, of which the criticism of television forms an integral part. Everybody is a television critic. I have never met anybody who wasn't. The only difference is that a few of us write it down.

THE
CRYSTAL
BUCKET

Hitler's faults

ALBERT SPEER has a new book out and turned up on *Newsday* (BBC2) to plug it. As usual, his air of bewildered humility served him well, despite some fairly close questioning from Ludovic Kennedy.

As we already knew from previous appearances, Speer is willing to be contrite about Nazi atrocities, but only on the understanding that he knew very little about them. Undermining Speer's position on this point is the fact that as Hitler's armaments minister he was necessarily one of the best-informed men in Germany. Nevertheless his puzzled frown has remained firmly in place, throughout his stretch in Spandau and on into sweet liberty. Time goes by, people forget, but Speer is too canny ever to forgive himself out loud. By now he probably sincerely believes that he didn't know quite what was happening to the Jews. It all came as a huge disappointment to him.

But when Ludo pressed that very point, Speer dropped *eine kleine* clanger. 'I can't say I didn't know it had happened,' he conceded. A civilised moment of hesitation, and he continued: 'I was only astonished by *how* it had happened ... the way it was done.' If this meant anything, it meant that Speer knew the Jews were being wiped out, but *thought that they were being wiped out in some acceptable way.* Ludo was content to leave Speer's utterance hanging in the air, having rightly judged it to require no comment. If Speer couldn't see that he had been self-revealing, there was no point telling him.

In Spandau, Speer had had 'quite a good connection with Rudolf Hess'. Another moment of hesitation, and then once again the delicious qualifier: *'Despite all the differences we had in the political field.'* According to Speer, there were two parties among the incarcerated hierarchs. One party saw Hitler as having been without 'faults'. The other party could see that

Hitler had had 'faults'. Speer quietly aligned himself with the second party. One almost found oneself nodding understandingly.

Yes, Speer would have us believe, he had known a thing or two. He hadn't been that easy to fool. On the other hand, he would also have us believe, he hadn't known a thing or three. He hadn't been that *difficult* to fool. After all, how else had Hitler swung that business about the Jews except by exploiting the natural, human gullibility of men like Speer?

That, at any rate, was the impression Speer strove to conjure up, speaking very slowly, not so much because his English is rudimentary as because his mouth was full of butter, which was not melting. He came over – he has always come over – as a charming, even nice, bloke. Though his quarrels with Hitler probably sprang more from impatience at counter-productive imbecility than from outrage at moral squalor, there is no reason to think that Speer was devoid of a sense of right and wrong. He just didn't have *much* of a sense of right and wrong. But to judge him even to that extent is to evince dangerous confidence, unless we are very sure that we would have behaved better ourselves.

14 March, 1976

Mutiny in the Furnace Room

'WELCOME, mighty potentate,' said Vultan of Sky City to his Imperial Majesty Ming the Merciless of Mongo, Emperor of the Universe. 'If we had been informed of your coming, a banquet would have been served!'

The high point of the Bicentennial celebrations on television, last weekend's compilation of all the episodes from the forty-year-old *Flash Gordon* serial (BBC1), was full of such classic lines. 'Mutiny in the Furnace Room!' cried one of

26

Vultan's winged lieutenants as Flash, played with incomparable awkwardness by Buster Crabbe, battled his way out of durance vile, only to be recaptured and forced to combat the unspeakable Mighty Beast of Mongo for the chill hand of Dale Arden, while oddly continuing to reject the blandishments of Ming's hotcha daughter, Princess Aura. Ming in his turn was keen on Dale. Sweating it out under the mangy fur, the actor inside the Mighty Beast costume was the legendary Ray 'Crash' Corrigan. Flash, Crash, Mongo, Ming. It worries me that I possess this information.

But nothing defines an historical period like its vision of the future, and *Flash Gordon*, with its thick hero, mad villains, cheap props and clumsy innocence, remains a useful pointer to how simple the world must have seemed in 1936. Switch on *Dr Who* (BBC1) and you can't tell the heroes from the heavies, it's all so sophisticated. 'You've reached the point where your tissues are so massively hybridised that the next metabolic change could be the final one,' Dr Who tells his friend. Imagine getting Buster Crabbe to deliver a line like *that*. It would have taken a week.

Similarly the technology has made giant strides towards authenticity. When Flash's pal Dr Zarkov talked nonsense, it sounded like nonsense. When Dr Who talks nonsense, it sounds like Science. 'He's been infected with anti-matter. His brain cells have been destroyed. He'll descend to the level of a brute!' Dr Zarkov wouldn't have known anti-matter from his elbow: he just concentrated on running up a 'new ray' out of old torch batteries so that Flash could blast the Lion Men's Gyro-ship out of the sky and rescue Dale.

11 July, 1976

The weld this week

I T was cool-blowing time for David Dimbleby on *Panorama* (BBC1). Drained of strength by a succession of all-night election specials, David was in no condition to make a smooth job of covering technical cock-ups.

Obeying Finagle's First Law of Engineering (which states that if anything can go wrong, it will) the cock-ups promptly occurred. David did a brief linking spiel into a film on Rhodesia. The film on Rhodesia rolled without sound. He tried again. This time the film on Rhodesia failed to roll at all. Temporarily abandoning the film on Rhodesia, David did a brief linking spiel into the other billed item, a film on the IMF. The film on the IMF failed to roll. The screen was occupied with nothing but David.

Here was his opportunity to tell us the story of his life. Here, at any rate, was his chance to do better than Sheridan Morley did when the same thing happened to him. (Sherry addressed the camera for ten solid minutes, saying nothing except 'The film … has … broken down. We … are waiting.') David's phone rang. It said something to him that he didn't want to hear. 'Does that mean', he asked incredulously, 'that you don't have film of either the IMF *or Rhodesia*?' He put the phone down and turned to the lens. The *Panorama* audience was at the other end of it, begging for a sign.

What could he say? Punch-drunk from days and nights of pretending to be interested in Miss Lillian and Walsall North, he was bereft of inspiration. His heart ached, and a drowsy numbness pained his sense. Eventually he began to speak, his sentences cast in some spacious epic measure, with heavy sighs marking the caesuras. 'We sit in silence. Hmm. Hope you stick with BBC1. Aangh. While we sort this out.' As if the sirens were singing in his ear-piece, his tongue grew thick and ceased to move. Telephone. 'Hello? OK.'

David wheeled back to camera and said 'I'm sorry,' but already his voice and image were fading. It was the Rhodesia film, returning as capriciously as it had departed. It was a good film, too, reminding us with some force that the white Rhodesians consider they have more than just material reasons for protecting their way of life.

But despite the Rhodesia film's sinister message, the thing that stayed in the mind was the spectacle of little David and his struggle against the machines. Usually it is only when they go wrong that machines remind you how powerful they are, how much they can do. One of the reasons people want to spend their lives in television is the beauty of the technology, the thrill of walking into the production gallery and seeing all the heaped jewellery of big and little lights, with the sound and vision engineers sitting in a row like the crew of an airliner a mile long.

Just the colours are enchanting: there is one kind of waveform display, expressing the picture information as a curve of light, which is the delicious green of emerald juice. The whole deal is a treat for the eyes: Science Fiction City! And before long you are armed with all kinds of jargon ('Give me a buzz when you're up to speed') and have persuaded yourself that you know what's going on. *But you don't know what's going on.* Only about two people in the entire building can really understand how the toys are put together. And the subject of Brian Gibson's marvellous *Horizon* programme *Billion Dollar Bubble* (BBC2) was what happens when those two people turn crooked.

Their field of operations, of course, was not television but computers. The story really happened, in America: a giant insurance company manufactured thousands of phoney policies in its computer and raised money on them – tangible assets whose tangibility was an illusion. The fraud was possible at all only through the compliance of a couple of young experts who knew how the policies could be made to hide inside the computer's memory so that the auditors wouldn't notice.

Gibson and his writer, Tom Clarke, did wonders in getting the actors to speak and act authentic Watergate. Senior executives talked of the company's need to 'generate some cash' in order to get over a 'temporary difficulty'. Nobody ever mentioned theft. In fact the mogul at the top of the heap echoed Nixon in being apparently unable to realise that anything wrong was going on at all. Meanwhile Art, the uptight young computer whizz, had allowed his loyalty to the company to overwhelm his regard for the law of the land. You couldn't help being reminded of the young lawyers who thought Nixon outranked the Constitution.

The deal came unstuck for two reasons. The first was Art's pal Al, the hang-loose young computer whizz. Unlike the responsibly irresponsible Art, Al, zonked on the dreaded weed, was irresponsibly irresponsible. Goofing off and fouling up, he blew security. But the second reason was built in: the fraud had to keep growing in order to stay intact, until finally the number of phoney people in the computer would have to outnumber the entire population of the United States. 'The bigger it gets the bigger it has to get to keep paying for itself each year.' It was wildly funny, intensely gripping viewing to watch the bubble swell. When it burst, all you could see were sad faces covered with soapy spray. The geniuses had assumed that since the people inside the computer didn't exist, nobody could get hurt. They had assumed wrong. *They* got hurt. Just because the caper was hygienic didn't make it clean.

Here corruption had been made funny without being trivialised. Probably it is only in free countries, however, that a humorous regard for corruption is possible. In the totalitarian countries, corrupt from top to bottom, nobody is laughing because nothing is laughable. There is no difference between what things are and what things ought to be, since what things ought to be no longer exists even as a standard. Hence the dreadful gloom attendant on *The Memory of Justice* (BBC2), a Marcel Ophuls blockbuster dedicated to preserving the memory of the Third Reich in all its moral significance. Ophuls's passion is admirable but his chances of success are small: it is all too hideous to be imagined by succeeding generations and one doubts that the capacity to imagine it would be much of a safeguard against its repetition.

Mad old Nazis were to be heard deploring modern decadence. 'The difference is, we weren't obsessed with smut,' said one comfortable retired SS man, all unaware of being up to his neck in blood and pus. Speer was once again in evidence, by now word-perfect in his role as the puzzled artist.

In *I, Claudius* (BBC2) Caligula ate Drusilla's baby. For those with stronger stomachs, however, Noele Gordon was on *Stars on Sunday* (Yorkshire), persuading us, in a heart-wrenching tremolo, of the necessity to keep striving, 'whatever differences there might be between the various races in this weld'. But another religious programme showed that the holy spirit retains at least a flicker of life: the *Anno Domini* report on Paraguay (BBC1) was eloquent about the horrors going on there and the bravery of those who resist.

14 November, 1976

The truly strong man

As a climax to the salutary dust-up caused by his book on Unity Mitford, David Pryce-Jones was on *Tonight* (BBC1), face-to-face with Sir Oswald Mosley. Referee: Melvyn Bragg.

As always, the streamlined head of Sir Oswald looked simultaneously ageless and out of date, like some Art Deco metal sculpture recently discovered in its original wrappings. Nor have his vocal cords lost anything of their tensile strength during the decades of enforced inactivity. Devoid of any capacity for self-criticism, Sir Oswald is never nonplussed when caught out: he simply rattles on with undiminished brio.

So vivacious a revenant was a difficult opponent for Pryce-Jones, looking about eight years old, to deal with. He didn't do so badly. There were about a hundred times he might have used his erudition to point out that Sir Oswald was talking grotesque malarkey, but that would have entailed finding some legally acceptable method of getting Sir Oswald to shut up. As it was, our brave young author did the next best thing. Apart from providing some useful quotations from Sir Oswald's pre-war speeches, he just sat back and let his interlocutor's much-touted political savvy reveal itself for what it actually is.

Sir Oswald was bent on establishing that Unity's life was 'a simple, tragic story of a gel who was what we called stagestruck in those days' and that Pryce-Jones, in writing a book about such of her little quirks as anti-Semitism and blind adoration of Hitler, had done nothing but stir up trouble. Married to one of the Mitford sisters, Sir Oswald was outraged on behalf of the family. In addition, he took exception to being described as anti-Semitic himself. Unity might have been anti-Semitic, but that was madness. Hitler might have been anti-Semitic, but that was Nazism. *He*, Sir Oswald, had never been anti-Semitic. Nor had his movement, the British Union of Fascists – which, to hear Sir Oswald tell it, must have been some kind of philanthropic organisation.

Already slightly exophthalmic even in repose, Pryce-Jones was bug-eyed at the magnitude of Sir Oswald's gall. To know that the shameless old spell-binder had been peddling these whoppers for years is one thing. To have him produce them right there in front of you is another. Purporting to counter Pryce-Jones's allegation that he had sent a thank-you note after being congratulated on the impeccability of his sentiments by Julius Streicher, Sir Oswald defined Streicher as 'a man I had absolutely nothing to do with'. The thank-you note had been a stock answer, nothing personal.

Pryce-Jones tried quoting chapter and verse to show that the message in question had been from the heart, but there was no way for the viewer to judge. With the details so far in the past, it was Pryce-Jones's word against Mosley's. What Pryce-Jones forgot to mention, for the benefit of those in the audience who don't realise what Sir Oswald's word on these subjects is worth, was the fact that Julius Streicher was a murderous, raving anti-Semite whose pornographic fantasies were already official Nazi policy by the time Sir Oswald sent his note. *Any* kind of thank-you to Streicher was a clearly recognisable anti-Semitic act.

But you will never catch Sir Oswald admitting to anti-Semitism. All he does is embody it. He talked of 'the use of Jewish money power to promote a world war'. Taxed on this point, he disclaimed anti-Semitism by saying that he meant 'not all Jews, but some Jews'. That's as far as he will ever reduce his estimate. The truth, of course, is that the real number of Jews responsible for World War II was zero. Pryce-Jones tried to say something along those lines, but Sir Oswald shifted ground, saying that he himself had made anti-Jewish speeches only after the Jews started 'attacking our people on the streets'. Like Hitler, Sir Oswald obviously regarded any resistance on the part of an innocent victim as provocation.

'I object to this issue being raised now,' Sir Oswald hammered on, oblivious to the fact that this issue has never gone away. As if to prove that it hasn't, he had the hide to claim that the Jews would have been as safe as houses in Germany if they had not been so foolish as to promote the war. Before the war, apparently, Dachau had been like Butlin's. If the Jews had really been in peril, then 'why did they not leave Germany?' Here Pryce-Jones, or Bragg for him, should really have told this terrifically silly man not to blaspheme.

Mosley contends that to rake these things up can only injure national unity. 'The quarrel', he announced brazenly, 'has been over for forty years.' Plainly he foresees a national

33

government, with himself at the head of it. That is what he has been hoping for through all these years of exile. He loves Britain and has been waiting for its call – all unawares that the best reason for loving Britain has always been its reluctance to call him, or anybody like him. If it had done nothing else but encourage Sir Oswald to expose himself, Pryce-Jones's book about Unity Mitford ('a sweet gel, an honest gel') would have performed a service.

In *I, Claudius* (BBC2) Caligula finally got his. John Hurt had a marvellous time in the role, poncing lethally about with lines like 'And now I must away to shed more light.' Perhaps inspired by Hurt's furiously camping presence, the scenes of dissipation, which earlier in the series tended to recall the Windmill, rose to approximate the standard set by Raymond's RevueBar. Which is probably what the originals were like, when you come to think about it. The famous horse made an appearance. 'His life has really opened up since I made him a senator.' It was clear that Caligula must have posed the same problem then that Idi Amin poses now: how to knock the mad bastard off. A question less ethical than practical. The contract having at last been filled, Claudius rose to power. A wonderful series, like a sexed-up version of *The Brothers* (BBC1), in which the big question now is whether April will get off with the Dutchman.

On *Miss World* (BBC1) Patrick Lichfield and Sacha Distel helped herd the beef. Even further down-market, *The Royal Variety Performance* (BBC1) was hosted by Max Bygraves, who tried the time-honoured gimmick of singing the finale at the start. 'And if you doan like our finish/You doan have to stay for the show.' Thanks. Click.

21 November, 1976

34

Patrick's invisible lute

FRESH back from a tour of the outer planets, Patrick Moore was on *Face the Music* (BBC2). Resident host was Joseph Cooper, he of the silent piano. As always when Patrick and Joseph are in conjunction, the results were spectacular.

The screen was ablaze with inexplicable phenomena. For example, Patrick was unable to recognise a portrait of the Queen. Admittedly the portrait was by Annigoni, but it did look *something* like her. It made you wonder about all those times on *The Sky at Night* when Patrick confidently assures you that the minuscule smudge in the bottom left-hand corner of the photograph is a quasar at the edge of the universe.

But the high point came when Patrick got into trouble over another question and Joseph tried to give him a hint. Giving a hint to Patrick isn't easy. The question involved identifying some musical instrument: a lute, if I remember rightly. Anyway, Joseph decided to mime that he was playing one of these.

Patrick, with his head in the Magellanic Clouds, did not catch on. Joseph increased his efforts, strumming frantically at the empty air. After the silent piano, the invisible lute! Patrick looked stumped. His face was a study – I mean on top of the study it is normally. Ask him about the period luminosity relation in cepheid variables and he knows where he is, but he is no good on invisible lutes. Joseph mugged and plucked. Patrick groaned and writhed. The viewer goggled in disbelief. Two great clowns were locked in combat. It was a needle-match for nutters, a Brands Hatch for buffoons, a demolition derby for dingbats.

Also on the panel, the new model Robin Ray remained calm. Calm was something the old model Robin Ray could never remain for a minute, but the years bring tranquillity even to the hysterical. The week before, on the same programme, Robin had failed to remember that the K-number of Mozart's 'Coronation' piano concerto is 537. There was a day when such a lapse would have sent him into paroxysms of defensive laughter. But this time he just sat there, silently smiling: a fatalist. Robin Ray has acquired *gravitas*, a presence befitting his new role as front-man for the programmes being put out under the catch-all title *The Lively Arts* (BBC2). Humphrey Burton's biggest project since he moved back to the Beeb, this series has already established itself, in my view, as a success.

And fronting most of its programmes is the new model Robin Ray. Only once has he fallen back on his erstwhile habits. After introducing a production, starring Teresa Berganza, of *The Barber of Seville*, he reappeared during the interval to help commemorate the composer by eating, with the help of his wife, some Tournedos Rossini prepared in the studio by the chef from the Savoy, or it could have been the Ritz. The chef from the Ritz, or it could have been the Savoy, explained the recipe step by step, for those of us in the audience who had a spare truffle within reach and were keen to have a go.

Robin clucked appreciatively between, and often during, mouthfuls. All this was numbingly trivial and had the sole merit of echoing with exactitude the merits of the opera itself — Mozart minus the brains. But apart from this one slovenly attempt to link high art with rich living (not only is there no connection, there's an active antagonism), *The Lively Arts* has kept a high average in which Robin and Humphrey could be excused for taking some pride.

28 November, 1976

Over the tarp

WITH *Cat on a Hot Tin Roof*, Granada's blockbusting series entitled 'The Best Play of 19—' really got under way. The previous week's Pinter piece had been but a curtain-raiser. Here was the main action, with a meaty part for Olivier as a southern fried patriarch.

Southern *frard* patriarch. The accent gets into your head. Whether the play itself does any more than get on your nerves is another question. I can remember being young enough, long enough ago, to believe that in Tennessee Williams the giant themes of Greek tragedy had returned, all hung about with magnolias. Ignorance of Greek tragedy helped in this view. This was the 1950s, when a lot of intentions were being taken for deeds.

Later on the illusions crumbled. The American theatrical revival was widely seen for what it was. But even when it became generally accepted that most of the Broadway post-war classics were, by thoughtful standards, clap-trap, it was still contended that they *worked*. You heard a lot about Tennessee Williams's plays *working*. And indeed it could still be contended that *Cat on a Hot Tin Roof works*, in the sense that it coheres and resolves instead of just falling apart.

But at what a cost. Principally to the listener's ear-drums. Even in this television production the actors had to shout as loudly as they would have had to do on stage, since if they lapsed even briefly into normal tones it would become apparent that every character in the play is doing all the time what normal human beings do only in rare moments of passion – i.e., say exactly what's on their minds. The convention of raw frankness can only be sustained if all concerned are in a permanent wax. So the actors rant. Rant on stage can look like powerful acting to the uninitiated, but on TV it looks like tat even to a dunce.

In these circumstances, Olivier's Big Daddy must be counted a triumph. He brought nobility to a role which hasn't really got any. Tennessee might have thought it did when he wrote it, but what he was counting on, even if he didn't realise it, was that you would remember broken kings in plays by other hands. His own broken king possesses no qualifications except a zillion acres of cotton to justify him in lashing out with his personality. But Olivier gave the role overtones of Oedipus, Coriolanus, Lear – almost enough overtones to cover up its undertones.

Students of theatrical arcania will know that in Tennessee's original version of the play Big Daddy did not come back on after the end of Act Two. The play's director, Elia Kazan, persuaded its author that if the play was to be a success Big Daddy would have to return. After the mandatory struggle with his artistic conscience, Tennessee succumbed to this request (Kazan was, after all, right: in plays that *work* stage-craft is everything) and brought Big Daddy back on, armed with a show-stopping dirty joke about an elephant's erection. Understandably eager to play the revised version, Olivier duly made his reappearance, but the joke was missing. It suddenly occurred to me that a lot else was missing: nearly every overt crudity in the play had been scrubbed.

So all those rumours had been true, about the American television executives ringing up Manchester and calling for deletions! There had also been rumours about the stipulated size of dressing rooms for Natalie Wood and Robert Wagner – requirements which allegedly entailed the knocking down of walls. From these premises Wood and Wagner sallied forth each day of production to incarnate Maggie the Cat and Brick the Thick respectively. They weren't all that bad. Maggie is the best part and Natalie made something of it, although light-weight actresses run short of variations when they go over the top – which, needless to say, she had to do. Try *under*playing lines like that and see where you get.

As for Robert, he did what Paul Newman did in the movie

version. He lurched around looking beautiful and damned. He hasn't aged a bit since *Beneath the Twelve Mile Reef*. The gorgeous teeth were kept concealed by turning the mouth down at the corners, thereby indicating the imminence of perdition. There is no limit to the sacrifices actors will make just to get near Olivier, and quite right too. The whole production was a spankingly neat surround for his magisterial talent.

In the first episode of BBC1's two-part *Lady of the Camellias* Kate Nelligan had to establish herself in a role whose possibilities you might be excused for thinking Garbo had exhausted. She did astonishingly well – helped, perhaps, by two temporal advantages. Liberal speech about sexual matters having come on a bit since Garbo made *Camille*, Miss Nelligan had better lines to say. And Garbo was not exactly in the first flush of youth, whereas Miss Nelligan is. Marie Duplessis, the original of Marguerite Gautier, was wise beyond her years, but her years were few.

Marie Duplessis was a kind of artist. Men of genius fell in love with her as with a fellow talent. There is scarcely a dissenting voice about her gifts. Arsène Houssaye called her a clever woman who talked nothing but nonsense (here I attempt to adduce one measly fact that was not in Glenys Roberts's excellent *Radio Times* article), but otherwise all were agreed that her company was magic and her love a benediction. Any actress who plays her is being asked to embody life itself. Not to fail in such a role is to succeed wildly. As for Peter Firth's Armand, he is wet where Robert Taylor was wooden. On the whole I prefer moisture to splinters.

The Shah of Iran was on *Panorama* (BBC1), telling David Dimbleby that his lucky citizens 'can express themselves absolutely freely within the framework of the Constitution'. With admirable toughness, David asked, 'Are you satisfied with the methods that SAVAK uses to get confessions?' The Shah replied: 'They are improving every day.'

19 December, 1976

Supermind, Superbody

JESUS, what a fortnight. I mention Him first only because He didn't get much of a look-in among the other festive-schedule superstars. Exposure-wise, He rated somewhere just below the runner-up in the final of *Mastermind* (BBC1) and just above David Steel in the *Liberal Party Political Broadcast* (all channels).

The *Mastermind* final was a nailbiter. Held in the Cambridge Union debating chamber, which Magnus Magnusson wrongly called 'the setting for many a stirring debate', it featured three men versus the Post Office lady whose weird head-bands had been fascinating the nation for months.

Does the wild head-gear help her think? That had been the question on everybody's lips as the winsome lass blasted her way to victory after victory. Is that thing on her head wired for sound? Has she got an accomplice outside with an *Encyclopedia Britannica* and a walkie-talkie? Whatever the truth of the matter, on the big night she appeared with nothing up there except hair. It was probably just co-incidence that she crashed to defeat, licked hollow by the bloke with the big ears. Goodbye baby and amen. So for once it was a chap who walked off with the glass trophy, dubbed by Magnus 'a glittering prize indeed'.

Thus it was that *Mastermind* was laid to rest, only to rise again a few days after with a new title. After *Mastermind*, *Supermind*! Once again on BBC1, once again staged in the Cambridge Union, this contest was described, once again by Magnus Magnusson, as 'a new-fangled battle of wits ... a searching examination of erudition ... ' and a lot of other stuff I didn't catch, overpowered as I was by the mere sight of the assembled mental giants.

Reading from left to right, these were Radio Brain of Britain, a Former Radio Brain of Britain, the 1976 Brain of

Mensa (presumably another planet), and Mastermind himself, none other than our friend with the ears. There were half a dozen different kinds of test but it was clear from square one that the Earthlings didn't stand a chance against the creature from Mensa. His antennae were taped flat against his head and covered with plastic make-up but that third nostril was a dead giveaway.

What use is a Supermind without a Superbody? That was the message of *The Superstars* (BBC1), an international contest for sporting all-rounders hosted by David Vine and Ron Pickering. The scene of the action was France, where the *pluie* was *pissant* down. David explained that the stuff falling out of the sky was rain. Ron backed him up with an on-the-spot report delivered from beneath an umbrella. 'As David Vine was saying, weather conditions are absolutely appalling.'

Ron interviewed a drowned rat who answered to the name of Gareth Edwards. 'I'm not looking forward to this at all,' said the Welsh rugby-player, eyeing Ron's umbrella with understandable envy. Edwards complained of a 'suspect hamstring' – the *in* injury of 1976 – but he, you, me and everybody except David and Ron were well aware that the only thing suspect was his head, for having allowed him to participate in the first place.

Empty grandstands glistening all around, Edwards ran an impressively slow 100 metres with only the top half of his body showing above water. Before the next event he had to go back and be interviewed again by Ron. 'How do you feel this time?' 'Not too enthralled.' By this stage the water was running out of my television set and all over the floor.

The John Curry Spectacular (LWT) was sport too, but of a kind tending towards art. Or at least art is what it tried to tend towards. Not for the first time in the world of silver blades, the art-thrill which sometimes emerges in the rigour of competition turned to kitsch in conditions of creative freedom. The production was brilliantly smooth but things kept

41

not coming to fruition. An orchestra sat on the ice (well, the chairs it sat on were on the ice) while Curry skated amongst them, but he would have skated better if they hadn't been cluttering up the rink and you couldn't help noticing the stretch of goose-pimpled shin between the cuffs of the oboeist's trousers and the top of his socks.

Peggy Fleming, who in competition was the finest artist yet to have appeared on skates, came out of retirement to join Curry in a wispy *pas de deux*. She has put on a couple of pounds around the stern but was otherwise as lovely as ever. Curry pretended to chase her through the woods. The question of what might have happened had he caught her remained academic.

The first part of a two-part *This Week* (LWT) grippingly plunged us into London's Underworld. Here was Soho Vice laid bare. It seems that back in 1956 a villain called Tommy Smithson got killed. The two characters who bumped him off are now out and ready, even eager, to talk. Catching Smithson alone without his bodyguards, they had no hesitation in going for him, even though the odds — a mere two to one — were far from favourable. Their gun jammed, but between them they got it working again, and eventually were in a position to shoot Smithson through the neck at a range of three inches.

2 January, 1977

Rings a bell

THE Queen, God bless her. *Panorama* (BBC1) got in with the first of the Jubilee specials. The emphasis was on a job of work well done.

Julian Pettifer, jaw staunchly thrusting, bore the main brunt of the interviews. Sir Alec Douglas-Home told him that the Queen was a good thing. Pettifer looked very tired in the cutaways, as if listening to a small, dull child reading aloud from Dr Seuss. Sir Harold Wilson was more exciting on the subject. 'She wants to know it all,' he exulted, his tiny eyes deliquescent with adoration. John Grigg, alias Lord Altrincham, pointed out that a lot of mutual admiration goes on between Buck House and No. 10. The Prime Minister of the day is always to be heard applauding the Queen's wisdom, but her role in his life is actually more therapeutic than advisory.

Back to Sir Harold, still working on the eternal problem of how to hold his unlit pipe. Up here? Down there? As always, it looked like a cheap prop whatever he did with it. Meanwhile, he was proclaiming himself sorry for Presidents. The Head of State should not also be Head of Government. This was a strong constitutional point. It was, after all, the existence of the monarchy which enabled Sir Harold to contemplate stepping down from the leadership. Otherwise he would have been compelled to go on looking after us for ever.

Lord Gardiner, avowedly no passionate devotee of the Throne, nevertheless argued persuasively for the Monarch's role in denying power to the ambitious. Here was the voice of sanity. Here, on the other hand, was Lord Hailsham, being fervent about the sort of thing you would get if the Monarchy were to be abolished. He conjured up 'the unknown, elastic-sided-booted members of the Third Republic'. He stuck his finger in his ear. There being no other depths left to plumb, the programme came to an end, with the credits rolling over the image of Lord Hailsham shouting, 'Hooray! Hooray! Hooray!'

Only a day later, *The Year She Came In* (Yorkshire) concerned itself with evoking the spirit of 1952. It was all too obvious that in the year the Queen succeeded the country was already failing. There was much talk of a new Elizabethan Age, but to hindsight, or hindhearing, it all blends in with the general hubbub of self-deception. The newsreel commentaries were especially revelatory. Conjuring vast fantasies of power and influence, the commentators probably did more than anything else to convince the outposts of Empire that the homeland was on its way down the drain.

Capably linking the film clips, Robert Kee wondered about what possible 'stature' Britain might usefully now seek. There are no easy answers, but surely it is permissible to suggest that the country is in far better psychological shape than it used to be. At least everyone knows the chips are down. The stuff Britain exports now, people actually want. In 1952 they took it because there was nothing else. The newsreel footage of the Standard Vanguard production line was particularly touching in this context. Out in Australia it was always a toss-up whether the Vanguard's chromium trim would rust through before the exhaust pipe fell on the road. The first Volkswagens were greeted like liberators.

Television, though. That's something else. Britain does well there. Look at the BBC. And indeed the Beeb is a great institution, always to be defended against its enemies, which include itself. There are many things Auntie does well, but the blockbuster science programme is not one of them. Often written by Nigel Calder, it tends to be elephantine in scope and redolent of the specious clarity which leaves you knowing less. *The Key to the Universe* (BBC2) was a good, or bad, example of the genre. The voice-overs were done by Eric Porter, as usual over-enunciating like Julie Andrews, but the man in vision was Nigel Calder himself, awkwardly poised on a studio-spanning suspension bridge, the stars his background. Several heavyweight scientists were interviewed. Natural talking heads, they were fascinating to hear, especially the Americans. Professor Murray Gell-Mann could get a job fronting *Tonight* any time, but unfortunately he prefers to fritter away his talent chasing quarks.

Explaining their theories with lucidity and charm, the scientists might have gone a long way towards helping you understand what a quark is, if Calder had not been there to

The way she tells it, the Festspielhaus enjoyed the favour of Hitler and the Party but apart from certain subsidies it still had to make its own way. There were no Nazi demonstrations in the auditorium, at Hitler's own request. She interceded for her Jewish musicians, forwarding petitions when asked.

The petitions were nearly always successful, thanks to her friendship with Hitler, about which she still has no qualms, since it was purely a human tie – no politics. She sounded tough yet reasonable. Here, you could imagine bright young viewers thinking, was one Nazi not entirely to be despised. Someone who had behaved rather well even though backing the wrong horse. Someone larger than her accusers.

It all happened a long time ago. Perhaps the guilty were a bit more innocent, the innocent a bit more guilty, than they were painted. Best to leave it alone. That, at any rate, is the ploy on which somebody like Albert Speer is relying: to sit there looking puzzled and regretful until nobody cares any more. But Winifred, to do her credit, is less devious than that. She sees no necessity to cover up, since she was right all along.

Her *Verhältnis zu Hitler*, being non-political, was the kind of relationship that could draw to the full on his reserves of 'Austrian human tact and warmth'. She called him 'Wolf' and he called her 'Wini'. Tiptoeing upstairs together on the Führer's frequent visits to Haus Wahnfried, Wolf and Wini cooed over the tots' cots. Apparently Adolf and the two Wagner boys (Wieland and Wolfgang, later to be Festival directors in their turn) addressed each other in the familiar form, *du*. So touching. But what about all those other children whose lives were being made Hell not far down the road?

It was on this point that Winifred's show of hard-bitten realism turned to mush. She has a point when she says that it is easy not to be a Nazi now that Hitler is no longer around. But she neglects to mention that there were a lot of people who were anti-Nazi even when he *was* around, simply because they could see him for what he was. She couldn't, or else didn't want to. According to Winifred, her children weren't saying *du* to the Devil, they were saying it to their country's redeemer. Look at the *Volksgemeinschaft* which Hitler gave Germany – the feeling that workers of all kinds were part of one movement. Bless his big, blue eyes, he towered above his offsiders. 'I except Hitler quite generally from that whole crowd.'

Especially she excepted him from Streicher. The whole Jewish issue was a bee in Streicher's bonnet. Apparently 'we all' thought Streicher an impossible piece of work. No, the Final Solution had little to do with Wolf and nothing at all to do with Wini. 'Nothing outside touched me.'

The first fallacy is obvious, or ought to be: men like Streicher didn't act independently of Hitler's will, they *were* his will. The second fallacy is harder to get at, but in the end more important. Winifred was fooling herself to imagine that nothing outside touched her. You can't keep a stench like that outside. It seeps into everything. Still, Winifred proves just how bright you can be without realising that you are participating in a nightmare.

Back in Britain, where politics tend to be a good deal quieter, Lady Falkender made a well-timed bed-of-pain appearance on ITN, disarming her critics by freely admitting that she had the occasional tantrum – and who wouldn't, after twenty years hard? A Joe-come-lately like Mr Haines could scarcely be expected to know what was involved. With this interview Lady Falkender scored a plus which not even Sir Harold Wilson could turn into a minus.

Making his own appearance on ITN a few days later (the Beeb was out in the cold), Sir Harold was stripped for action – no pipe. He referred to what Lady Falkender had said 'on the *Jimmy Young Show*'. He called himself 'a very resilient and relaxed character'. He referred again to what Lady Falkender had said 'on the *Jimmy Young Show*'. He was cunningly under-standing about Joe. But he made a gentle plea for reason. 'You're talking about molehills when my problems were mountainous.' Moses – the Lawgiver!

But perhaps the country isn't so badly governed after all. *The State of the Nation* (Granada) cast journalists as politicians in a compressed reconstruction of the Cabinet debates *re* the IMF loan. With Anthony Crosland at death's door, there was a case for postponing the programme, but Mrs Crosland bravely agreed to its transmission. As it happened, Crosland came out of it well. His unexpectedly trenchant arguments against cuts in social services were put by the best natural actor of the bunch, Peter Jenkins of the *Guardian*. David Watt played Callaghan. Everybody caught one another's eye with a 'Spot the loon' look when Benn was talking. The show was probably true to life, since each Minister had a vested interest in briefing the journalist chosen to play him. It's a sweet technique for getting at the truth, so I imagine someone will put a stop to it soon enough.

While Frank Finlay was having his stomach pumped – Yerk! Karf! Whark! – in *Another Bouquet* (LWT), his ritzy mistress Sarah piled into the palliasse with young Gavin, erstwhile lover of his wife Cassie and husband of his daughter Prue. In another part of the studio, Cassie was making it with Evan, medico father of Gavin's girl-friend Vicky. According to my pocket calculator, there is nobody left to get laid except the baby. Why am I watching such trash, when the small screen is yet rich with classics like *The Country Wife*? BBC1's Play of the Month, this was lavishly cast but stunningly dull, mainly because Wycherley's witticisms are not witty.

20 February, 1977

Moses hits the dirt

A ND Moses went up into the mountain, and he croaked. Thus ended *Moses – the Lawgiver* (ATV), just before it got really interesting.

So we never saw the Canaanites being slung out of Canaan. All we saw was Burt Lancaster promising his people yet another forty-year stretch in the wilderness. He and his generation had looked upon the promised land but were doomed never to set foot in it. Their transgressions had been too great. Not that Moses hadn't done his best to punish these. Manufacturers of the golden calf were obliged to melt it down and drink it, with deleterious results. Two characters who had broken the Sabbath by picking up twigs were stoned to death on the Lawgiver's orders. Their relatives thought this penalty harsh, but Moses was immovable. However hostle they might become, the Children of Israel must respect the Law, or they would never get to see the fertle land.

'When will father be coming? I want to see him,' pleaded one of Moses's offspring. 'He's very busy,' was the reply. 'He has Israel to look after.' Even at the nadir of his popularity, the Israelites still crowded round the Lawgiver to 'see con- struction', meaning seek instruction. At times like these he was wont to call them 'my foolish children'. Despite the un- avoidable anachronism of a set of teeth whose fearful sym- metry has been reflecting the sunlight like a heliograph since he first leapt to fame as the Crimson Pirate in 1952, Burt did a reasonable job of impersonating a patriarch.

His authoritative presence was reinforced by miracles. Dathan, a rat-faced heckler who had been stirring up trouble from the beginning of the series, was finally obliter- ated by a special effect. As a follow-up, Moses clobbered the Israelites with the aforesaid forty years' additional sentence. It was becoming increasingly hard to see why anybody should put up with him even for forty minutes, but before his credibility ran out there was just time to get him back up into the hills for a farewell chat with God.

The fact that God also spoke in Burt's voice permitted the charitable conjecture that Moses had been mentally dis- turbed all along. Some gory flashes-forward suggested that

49

Operation Canaan would nevertheless proceed on schedule. Burt hit the dirt. The titles rolled. It had not been a compassionate series. Nor is the Old Testament. The show was remarkably true to the spirit of the book – hence the chill.

Compassion came later in human history. Jimmy Reid personifies it. On *Opinion* (Granada) he gave us a cracking sermon about the obscenity of supposing that the Welfare State has achieved its objects and that poverty has disappeared. Reid has a finely developed idea of what society should be like. In some respects his vision of the good life outstrips his political theory. Too concerned with freedom to believe in absolute justice, and too concerned with justice to believe in absolute freedom, Reid is in a dilemma. But if it does nothing else, his mental turmoil makes him a breathtaking preacher.

'Far have I come, pursued by stormy weather,' sang *The Flying Dutchman* (BBC2). This was the second showing of a production which I had been lucky enough to miss on the first occasion. For some reason several critics had gone on record as believing it to have been television magic. Actually it was the kind of thing that gives opera a bad name. Just when the increased use of subtitles is beginning to give the viewing public a chance of overcoming the one big stumbling block that lies between them and the glories of the international operatic repertory, somebody puts back the clock by giving us Wagner in English. But what *kind* of English? 'My blood runs cold with nameless terror.'

Not having heard about Moses snuffing it, Magnus Magnusson was still pounding around the biblical landscape in *BC* (BBC2). This has been an enjoyable series, but Magnus seems to have put less time into the script than into booking airline tickets. Calling the Ten Commandments a 'social contract' was not only vulgar but confusing, since it explained the intelligible in terms of the unintelligible. But the latest episode, dealing with the Philistines, was full of stirring news. It appears that the Philistines, far from being arid materialists, were deeply artistic, with a terrific line in pottery. Proof of this talent was abundantly forthcoming. Boy, could they pot. Once again the Bible had got it all wrong.

'This was the sort of pillar that Samson is alleged to have pulled down,' said Magnus, bracing himself against a remain. Magnus demonstrated how the pillars in a Philistine temple stood at just the right distance apart for a man of Samson's presumably above-average dimensions to bring it crashing down on three thousand occupants. The only drawback to the story is that a Philistine temple, according to over-whelming archaeological evidence, was about the size of a modern living room. Which means, as far as I can see, that, at a generous estimate, he, Samson, wiped out thirty people —i.e., one-hundredth of the accredited total.

Introducing an item about architectural follies on *Nation-wide* (BBC1), Frank Bough used the 'I dunno' technique. 'I dunno what a folly is. Bob, what do you think a folly is?' Whereupon Bob Wellings chimed in with the equally reliable 'we asked' routine. 'Well, Frank, we asked an architectural expert what a folly is, and he told us what a folly is.' If these hallowed gambits are still found useful by *Nationwide*, per-haps they should be employed with equal vigour in other formats. Magnus, for example, might benefit from such an approach. 'I dunno what a Philistine is. Professor Moshe Bagelheim of Tel Aviv University, what do you think a Philistine is?' 'Vell, Magnus, ve asked ... '

Of the American fuzz operas currently on offer, *Serpico* (BBC1) is easily the best. The real Serpico moved in a world where all cops were bent except him. The fictional Serpico has a few good men on his side. On the other hand, no woman is against him. The real Serpico was a romantic, but surely not *that* romantic. Still, this is the story of a true hero, and stories of true heroes always grow in the telling. They pull down temples the size of telephone booths on the heads of three sensitive potters and by the time the book comes out there are three thousand victims.

Distressed viewers have written asking what to do now that *Bouquet* is off the air. Don't try to compensate with alcohol or drugs. Lie down, keep warm and wait for *The Brothers*.

27 February, 1977

Odour situation

INVESTIGATING some farmland which farmers say is polluted and the Department of the Environment says isn't, a reporter for *Nationwide* (BBC1) held out a jarful of earth to an inspector and asked him if he couldn't smell petrol. No, said the inspector, all he could detect was 'an environmental odour associated with petroleum'.

Can the English language be saved from a watery death? Not if the BBC2 linkmen can help it. You would think by now that everybody in the Land of the Media had got the message about the word 'situation'. Even Frank Bough is trying not to use it: when it springs to his lips he chokes it back, or covers it with a cough. But nothing gets through to the BBC2 linkmen. 'And now here's Michael Fish with the latest on the weather situation.'

If the language goes, everything goes. But perhaps everything is going anyway. Last week I accidentally-on-purpose never got round to saying anything about *Goodbye Longfellow Road* (Yorkshire) — it was just too discouraging to see such glaring evidence of the compassionate society failing to deliver the goods. But at least that programme dealt with something going wrong that could conceivably go right: the housing problem isn't necessarily insuperable, just immensely difficult. This week's shocker, *Spend, Spend, Spend* (BBC1), was about the inadequacies of a deprived personality, something impossible to mend. A drama-documentary written by Jack Rosenthal, it told a true story about a silly lady called

Vivian, whose even sillier husband, Keith, won £152,319 on the pools. They spent it in short order, hence the title.

One of the many strengths of the programme was that it didn't rush to judgment on the society which produced and destroyed Vivian and Keith. Certainly everything that happened to them, whether before or after their big win, was very nasty. But it was possible to imagine another couple scoring a comparable hoard and flourishing on it. All they would have had to be was less stupid.

Yet if stupidity is mainly just a lack of capacity to take things in, the blame could be laid squarely on upbringing. Flashbacks to the early home life of the fated lovers showed circumstances guaranteed to turn almost anyone into a shambling zombie. Prominent among these environmental factors was Keith's grandmother, not enough of whose head was wrapped in a scarf.

In this context, Vivian and Keith were more pitiful than frightening. That they were not more boring than pitiful was a tribute to Rosenthal's finely judged script, which caught the verbal squalor of Vivian's interior monologue without being either too perceptive to be true or too monotonous to be bearable. 'They say tomorrow never comes,' droned Vivian. 'They say there's no place like home.' Abandoning epigram for hyperbole, she described her early grapplings with Keith as 'The greatest sexual experience in the history of Castleford.'

Vivian and Keith were played, dead straight without a tinge of contempt, by Susan Littler and John Duttine: two admirable performances. Crowned by a variety of savagely backcombed hair-styles, weighed down by strings of fake pearls as big as ping-pong balls, Vivian lunged about desperately in her affluent dream, which had disappointed her the cruellest way it could – by coming true. It was a fearful show, redolent of death. Of an environmental odour associated with mortality.

More or less the same theme, but this time fully fictional-ised, was treated in the last episode of *Headmaster* (BBC2), a series which ended more strongly than it began, and ought to return. Not even Frank Windsor's all-seeing avuncularity was sufficient to halt the precipitous course towards doom of hideous little Stephen. Played by Mark Farmer, Stephen looked like Johnny Rotten of the Sex Pistols and behaved even worse, although more quietly. In time it was revealed that his noxious personality had a lot to do with regular beatings-up from his dad. But once again, just as in *Spend, Spend, Spend*, there was no sentimentality. You were struck with a mixture of emotions. Your first reaction was 'little bastard', your second was 'poor kid', and the best com-promise you could come up with was 'poor little bastard'.

Not to panic. In sport, Britain is still a world beater. Well, in some sports. For example, Britain always wins the Oxford–Cambridge boat race. There was an *Inside Story* (BBC2) on the 1976 Oxford eight. Stirring to see the old traditions so diligently upheld. Was at the other place myself, where it was always a thrill to hear that the hearties had celebrated a win on the river by burning their boat and throwing the porter's cat on the fire.

Salt of the earth, those men, and on this evidence we haven't run out of them yet. Rowing together makes them friends for life. 'I find it's a reasonable way of spending one's afternoons,' said one of the Oxford crew, an old Etonian, standing in the middle of his 4,000-acre estate. He had just shot something. Fairly soon he would shoot something else. Men of humbler origins seemed equally convinced that rowing gave you a sense of purpose. For one thing, it gave you a blue blazer to wear. A huge man of humble origins was shown taking delivery of his blazer. Now he would have a blazer to wear, to go with his oar on the wall! In Cambridge I never met a rower who did not have an oar on the wall. Win, draw, lose or sink, everyone got a prize.

Britain is still good at horses, too. I recommend a new

series called *Horses In Our Blood* (Yorkshire, some areas), narrated by Robert Hardy, a man of parts. It takes parts to ride a horse while simultaneously talking about 'the very great delight horses and humans have had for each other for thousands of years'. The horses' share of this delight has to be taken on trust, of course. Princess Anne, star of the first episode, was more matter-of-fact. She had never known a time when horses weren't part of the furniture. 'They were just there, and one got on them as one would have got on a bicycle.'

Robert laid much stress on 'the royal connection with horses', and Anne herself let slip something about 'contact in the stables', but to judge by the relevant footage HRH spends less time chumming up with the noble beast than in parting company from it. Ever and anon she crashed to the ground. What a jolly show though, and five more episodes to come. The air will be thick with the smell of horse-dung. With an environmental odour associated with equine bowel-movements.

20 March, 1977

The Lew Testament

THE Lord thy Grade hath done it again. After *Moses – the Lawgiver*, who else but *Jesus of Nazareth* (ATV)? Ring out the Old Testament, ring in the New.

And once again the results are not all that dire. This time the show is going out in two whopping chunks, the first last Sunday and the second tonight. Judging by the first three-hour half, Lord Grade has successfully reasserted his determination to handle these biblical matters with good taste. The director, Franco Zeffirelli, is in restrained form. There is no vulgarity. There is no sensationalism. In fact it gradually dawns on you that there is not much of anything, except good taste.

It would be straining at a gnat to laugh at the well-known thespian faces as they plug away at their starring roles, canter through as supporting players, or flare briefly on the screen in cameo appearances like those in *Around the World in Eighty Days*. After all, *somebody* has to play the parts, and unknowns couldn't manage. In Part One, Ralph Richardson was a suitably doddering Simeon who looked as if he might possibly drop the baby; Donald Pleasance, one of the Three Wise Men, was as wise as all get out; and Anne Bancroft realistically tarted herself up as the Magdalene.

Higher up the sanctity rankings, Michael York made a rugby-nosed firebrand out of John the Baptist. His teeth, like Burt Lancaster's as Moses, were probably too good to suit the time – I don't suppose there was much sugar around in those days, but there were no toothbrushes, either. Quibbles, these. You couldn't seriously fault the playing.

Even among the Holy Family, the casting has been thoughtfully done. Olivia Hussey, who once made a good Juliet for Zeffirelli, doesn't make a bad Mary, either. Of the 30-plus years she is supposed to age during Jesus's lifetime, she manages about three, but the Mother of God doesn't necessarily obey the same rules as other girls. The real trouble starts with Jesus Himself. Robert Powell plays Him with all the stops in. I have never seen an actor so heroically unforthcoming. In this fashion he goes a long way towards covering up the fact that nobody concerned with the show – whether Zeffirelli, the script-writers (Anthony Burgess once again heads the list) or Lord Grade on high – has made up his mind about what a Messiah actually *is*. Is it a man? Is it a bird?

Gothically concave of cheek, Powell's Jesus gives fireside chats, like J. B. Priestley during WW II. Oodles of serenity, but not a hint of nimbus. When the disciples stare deep into his eyes the reaction-shots show them to be overwhelmed by something or other, but it can't be charisma. More likely it is Positive Thinking. Nor are the miracles played up. On the contrary, they are played so far down they almost vanish. Nothing supernatural is allowed to obtrude. Even the Annunciating Angel is just a beam of light.

A very pretty beam of light. As so often happens with Zeffirelli, the design is the true hero. The exteriors, washed out like a tinted engraving, look eaten up by sunlight. The interiors echo Rembrandt's idea of glimmers in the gloom: scenes of dissipation in Herod's palace might have been hand-painted in Amsterdam, right down to the blobs of gold impasto. Zeffirelli can still handle crowds and costumes as surely as he ever did in his movies of *La Bohème* and *The Taming of the Shrew*, while the same soft powdery atmosphere the characters breathe in *Romeo and Juliet* is breathed in this.

Dusty mist and misty dust – it's the Zeffirelli Look. But the feeling of a revolution being worked in human affairs is lost among the cataracts of tact. Compare Pasolini's *The Gospel According to St Matthew* and you can see how Christ, without being made a shouting zealot, can nevertheless be shown to have come with a sword. Believers can reconcile His divinity with His humanity, and doubters can make a subject out of the difference. In this production there is neither belief nor doubt. As a consequence, only the rationalist element is transmitted with any real force. But there is enough of that to be going on with, and on the whole it can be said that this was a project well worth trying, especially when you consider how lousy those Hollywood biblical epics used to be.

Still on the subject of saving the world, but shifting the temporal focus to the present day, BBC1 devoted most of an evening to *The Writing on the Wall*, which turned out to be yet another episode in a continuing saga: Lord Chalfont Warns the West. Although the impression remains that Lord Chalfont is a little man with a big issue, it must be said that he came out of this programme sounding more authoritative than you might have expected. In a similar show for Anglia last year he was to be seen in the company of some of Britain's silliest right-wingers and to be heard propounding the necessity of giving up some of our freedoms in order to meet the Russian threat. Nor has he been slow to argue that in order to hold back the Communist tide we must learn to love the Shah.

Lord Chalfont might very well be right about Russian intentions, but he has a bad habit of overcooking his minatory tone. This time, however, he kept himself under tight rein. Even General Alexander Haig tried hard to sound normal. Speaking 'in the context of the broad trends', the General didn't want to paint too dark a picture of NATO's weakness. 'I reject the more extreme articulations,' he announced. On the other hand he didn't underestimate the threat.

Vladimir Dunaev of Russia rebutted Chalfont's claim to have presented an 'objective Western view', saying that a view had to be either Western or objective, but couldn't be both. Russia, Dunaev argued, persuasively, had good historical reasons for pointing a lot of tanks at Germany: it was a defensive stance, not an aggressive one. Chalfont fought back with some strong evidence about Russia's arms build-up. He was on weaker ground when stressing the menacing nature of Russia's civil defence programme, but by and large he stayed cool.

Only once did the pot crack. Would a Communist Government of Italy, he wondered, relinquish power if voted out? The implication being that a Communist Government ought not to be allowed in, even if elected. The train of thought will be familiar to students of Dr Kissinger – now, for a mercy, no longer in a position to run around destabilising Governments on our behalf.

Jesus couldn't do it, Lord Chalfont can't do it, but *Six Million Dollar Man* (Thames) did it – he saved the world. Forn agents turned a carnival into a rabbit worn of electronic devices in order to sabotage the B1 bomber, but Six nixed them with his bionic strength.

10 April, 1977

58

Roots of our time

'I AM caught between my desires and their frustray-hay-shun,' somebody sang in *A Child of Our Time* (BBC2), the renowned oratorio by Sir Michael Tippett. It was one of the big productions over Easter weekend.

The principal singers, clad in black and silver caftans looking like something William Cameron Menzies designed for *Things to Come*, and the chorus, neatly attired in black roll-neck ensembles vaguely suggesting *1984* – i.e., precisely evoking 1948 – were to be seen inhabiting a variety of symbolic settings. If they stood in white boxes, that meant they were being politically oppressed. Meanwhile, film clips of various low moments in modern history were copiously employed to reinforce the libretto, which, like all other verbal creations from Sir Michael's own hand, was serious, complex and unspeakable. It was singable only on the tacit assumption that it doesn't matter if what is sung sounds ludicrous.

It takes talent to generate triviality on the scale of *A Child of Our Time*. Sir Michael has some insight into concrete experience, but he also has pretensions to abstract thought. Dealing with the mass sufferings of the modern era, he is presented with so much concrete experience that he feels justified in treating it in an abstract manner. From that initial blunder, everything else follows – the caftans, the roll-neck sweaters, the portentous sets and the sententious lines. The oratorio ends on a 'personal' note of Hope, indicating that Sir Michael hasn't understood the blasphemy inherent in even flirting with the notion that the innocent dead suffered to some purpose.

But it doesn't matter, you might say, that a man in a black caftan standing in a white box should be heard to announce that he is caught between his desires and their frustray-hay-shun, so long as the music has substance. Unfortunately most of the substance in the music was second-hand, since the melodies originally belonged to Negro spirituals. What Sir Michael provided, apart from a goodly number of lines about desire and frustray-hay-shun, was mainly just the orchestray-hay-shun. At the fag-end of a tradition, the essential is seen as superfluous: nobody will mind if your building-blocks are borrowed. Sir Michael borrowed his from the blacks.

Which brings us naturally to *Roots* (BBC1). I have taken such a roundabout path only to provide an illustrative example for the contention that anaemic high art is less worth having than low art with guts. It could be said that *Roots* is as low as art can get. It could even be said that it isn't art at all. But guts it's got.

The series was such a success in America that a reaction had already set in among some of our pundits even before it reached this country. But accusations of commercialism and fakery don't really stand up. The series might be coining millions now, but when the idea was first mooted there was no guarantee that it would make a dime — like most previous all-black projects for screens large or small, it might have died in its own length. As for the question of authenticity, I don't see how it matters much that the author might have fooled himself into thinking his ancestry could be traced. If it was wishful thinking, it sprang from the very passion for identity that the story is about.

And anyway, *something* like this happened. In fact we can be sure that the scale and intensity of the cruelty were beyond anything that the script tries to convey. *The Fight Against Slavery*, currently being repeated on BBC2, shows you the scope of the crime. What *Roots* gives you is not scope but focus. The driving force comes less from the thoughts of the descendants of the criminal than the feelings of the descendants of the victim. Hence the anger which keeps the story alive, even when the details are unsatisfactory.

It has been objected that the African village in the first episode seemed to be inhabited exclusively by philosophers.

Certainly you couldn't help suspecting that the older villagers were unnaturally imbued with an ironic sense of humour concerning the doings of the younger: the jokey warmth recalled *Meet Me in St Louis*. Nevertheless the turn was well enough served, since we got the message we needed to get – that the villagers were the flower of their culture, whereas the slavers were the dregs of theirs.

As Kunta Kinte went through the tests of manhood (the circumcision ceremony providing a flinch-worthy moment for male viewers), the slave-ship ominously sailed towards landfall. It was as sure as fate that Kunta Kinte, bravest of the brave, would be snatched away from the life he was born for. You would have given a lot to stop that happening.

For the rest of the series the hero was in another world, where it was made very clear that the true savagery was all on the part of the civilised. The standard of the direction varied from episode to episode, but the performances were nearly all good and the script never faltered, even when its language was anachronistic. On the whole *Roots* is an achievement for America to be proud of. There can be no doubt that it will have a profound effect on the way Americans view their past. No large claims need be entered for the power of art to affect the world. But it is never wise to underestimate the power of a *story*. People who couldn't begin to understand *A Child of Our Time* will have no trouble remembering what happened to Kunta Kinte.

17 April, 1977

My daughter Tricia

'Do you feel that you ever obstructed justice, or were part of a conspiracy to obstruct justice?' asked David Frost in the first of *The Nixon Interviews* (BBC1), 'Well, in answer to that question ... ' Nixon began, and straight away you knew that an answer was the one thing the question would never get.

'As far as my information is concerned ... Let me say as far as what my motive was concerned ... my motive was not to try to cover up a criminal action ... but to be sure that as far as any slip-over ... or should I say slop-over ... it was that that I certainly wanted to avoid,' Nixon explained. 'If a cover-up is for the purpose of covering up criminal activities,' he went on, 'it is illegal. If, however ... I didn't believe we were covering up any criminal activities ... I was trying to contain it politically.'

Since Nixon has always belonged in show-biz rather than politics, Frost is to be commended for giving him this late start in his true career. Apart from the consideration that Frost is much nicer, the two men are remarkably similar: they are both essentially role-players. At a level too deep for speech, they understand each other well. Frost knew that he could talk as toughly as he liked and Nixon would go on sitting there. Nixon knew that he could talk any nonsense that came into his head and Frost would still not call the deal off. Neither man is capable of doubting that an historic occasion should be a performance.

While Frost played Grand Inquisitor, Nixon played the great statesman who had been brought down by his own compassion. He should have been ruthless with his lieuten-ants. It was largeness of heart, not smallness of mind, that undid him. 'Could I take my time now to address that ques-tion?' he asked, and straight away you knew that another Checkers speech was on its way around the S-bend towards you. 'It wasn't a very easy time ... I think my daughter Tricia ... '

As if he had not yet been overweening enough, Frost aban-doned the role of Grand Inquisitor and took on the greatest characterisation of all – God. He called upon Nixon to make a clean breast of it, or else face eternal damnation. 'Unless

you *say* it, you're going to be haunted for the rest of your life.'
This was a large assumption, since there are at least three
decades of evidence to suggest that Nixon is a hard man to
haunt.

As was inevitable, Nixon responded to the ultimate request
by accepting the responsibility and refusing the blame. Or it
could have been that he accepted the blame and refused the
responsibility – it was difficult to tell. What was certain was
that while admitting everything he was admitting nothing. 'I
want to say right here and now ... I said things that were
not true ... most of them were *fundamentally* true on the big
issues ... ' The ground having been prepared, he poured his
heart out all over it. 'Yep, I let the American people down.'
He let them down, you see, by allowing a silly little mistake
to deprive them of his services.

It still hasn't occurred to him that he let them down by
running for office in the first place. 'My political life is over
... maybe I can give a little advice from time to time.' As the
titles came up, the lingering impression was of a man who
had been brought low by circumstances. The fault, dear
Brutus, is not in ourselves, but in our stars. Therefore let us
weep upon the whole world's shoulder, and collect one million dollars in front, plus 10 per cent of the gate.

So if the first of the Frost–Nixon encounters was a television
non-achievement, what is a television achievement? There
are as many answers as there are examples – i.e., not all that
many. But *Vienna: The Mask of Gold* (BBC2) was certainly one
of them. Written and presented by Michael Frayn as a
companion piece to his excellent programme on Berlin, it
evinced all the same virtues plus the additional one conferred
by the sheer richness of Vienna's intellectual and creative
life.

Once again Frayn was analysing a city through its culture,
but whereas Berlin's culture had been mainly provincial,
Vienna's was of international class in every field. At ease with
the great names, Frayn paced out the dimensions of the

propinquitous village they all inhabited: Schoenberg, Karl Kraus, Freud, Mahler, Klimt, Schiele, Wittgenstein. 'It's a small world. Or rather, it's just the right size.' Mahler, Klimt and Kokoschka had had more than just talent in common. They had had Alma Mahler. Sexuality, Frayn made clear, was the factor that made the whole scene throb.

As proof of this thesis, a gallery of Klimt lovelies filled the screen – high-born ladies whose lustrous eyes and moist mouths suggested that the life which had given them everything had been empty until they met Klimt. Somewhere else in the picture, death looked on. In Schiele's pictures death ate the women up from inside. Trotting around the Ringstrasse in a fiacre, gumshoeing discreetly through Freud's house in the Berggasse, Frayn talked of a 'nagging sense of discrepancy between appearance and reality'. He has the rare gift of anchoring propositions to facts.

8 May, 1977

The Red Sandwich

A T the risk of boring you stiff, I'm honour-bound to deal with the awkward fact that in the subsequent *Nixon Interviews* (BBC1) David Frost did rather better than in the first one.

If the interviews had been screened in their correct order with the Watergate episode coming last instead of first, Frost would have been clearly seen to have started off quite impressively, and Nixon would have arrived at the finishing line so thoroughly compromised that Frost's relatively cursory treatment of him at the end would have looked like elementary tact.

Cambodia and Chile do, after all, matter a great deal more than Watergate. As it happened, burgling a hotel turned out to be an impeachable offence, whereas flattening whole countries and delivering their populations into the hands of torturers could be palmed off as diplomacy. But in the long run it is the second kind of activity which has the most penetrating moral resonance. Frost, to give him his due, could see this.

Nixon, of course, couldn't. In the second programme, largely devoted to his supposed triumphs in the field of what Frost (with increasingly Kissingeresque elocution) called diblomadic relations, Nixon talked grandly of how he had faced up to Brezhnev and Mao. Rare film footage was interpolated to prove that facing up to Mao in his last phase could have been no easy matter, the Chinese leader having come to resemble an indeterminate pile of flesh. The face was probably somewhere near the top. Nixon was to be seen shaking what was doubtless Mao's hand.

In the third show, however, Frost moved the area of discussion to South-East Asia, and immediately Nixon started looking shifty. Inevitably he fell back on his trusty technique of insisting that the course he took was the difficult one. He could have done the easy thing, but he did the difficult thing. (You will remember that even at the eleventh hour of his Presidency he was still doing the difficult thing – staying – instead of the easy thing – going.) Questioned on Vietnam, Nixon said that it would be easy now to say it was all a mistake, but he preferred to do the difficult thing and say that it had to be done.

Justifying the invasion of Cambodia, Nixon was unrepentant – the difficult thing. 'It was one of the most effective operations of the war.' Frost knew enough to insist that whatever the Cambodia caper had been, it had not been that. Nixon referred to 'a mass of offences' (i.e., a massive offensive) that the enemy had been about to launch. Frost suggested that the whole adventure had been a moral disaster as well as a military one. Nixon, as usual, didn't get the point. 'The cost of Cambodia was very high at home ... the Kent State thing.'

Frost, who had a sounder idea than Nixon about what the cost at home had been, asked about black-bag burglaries. Nixon admitted that such measures had been unpleasant – the difficult thing – but asked Frost to consider whether Roosevelt would not have been justified in assassinating Hitler during the 1930s. The effrontery of this argument left even Frost speechless.

And so to the last programme, in which Frost did his best to convince Nixon that on the question of Chile the fact that Allende had been voted into power, and that the United States had connived at removing him from office by illegal means, made Nixon's claim to have been defending democracy questionable at the very least.

Once again, Nixon didn't seem to get the point. Certainly he hadn't enjoyed supporting right-wing regimes – the difficult thing – but the fact remained that such regimes, whatever they did internally, did not export revolution, whereas left-wing regimes did. Nixon couldn't see then, and obviously still can't see now, that the alleged realism with which the US supported the Right was always the very thing which gave the Left its impetus.

If Nixon had any merit it lay in embodying the absurdity of a foreign policy which by Kissinger's sophisticated intelligence might otherwise have been made to look convincing. When Nixon spoke of 'the Red Sandwich' – the idea that Chile and Cuba between them might have subverted the whole of Latin America – Frost yodelled in derision. It was the first spontaneous thing he's done on television for years. Four hours of double-talk was a long way to go for a single magic moment, but when it came it was one to treasure. Nixon and the Red Sandwich!

All You Need Is Love (LWT) has been a long haul as well, but once again this is a case of a series turning out to be more valuable than it looked at first. The episode before last was particularly interesting, since it featured a good deal of dry talk from Derek Taylor, the best dry talker in the music business.

The latest programme, about rock's decline, came from the grandiloquent pen of Tony Palmer himself. Jimi Hendrix balling his guitar looked fearfully trite in retrospect. There was sad footage of Jim Morrison, so stoned that his eyeball pointed straight up through the top of his head. All such a waste. But that famous clip of an open-mouthed Mama Cass digging Janis Joplin's act at Monterey still arouses the old joy, if you can manage to forget what happened to both of them.

A *Lively Arts* (BBC2) on the Dance Theatre of Harlem was delectable. The combination of classical technique and the ability to boogie makes for a violently intoxicating rhythmic cocktail. The girls were enough to set even a eunuch moaning low. The viewer had no reason to be ashamed of sexism, since the company avowedly thrives on that very impulse: some of the male dancers joined up because they were caught girl-watching through the studio sky-light and told either to go away or join in.

According to *London Heathrow* (BBC1), the airport of that title was originally designed for half a million passengers a year. Now 23 million pass through. 90,000 meals a day are loaded aboard the planes. Each Jumbo yields three quarters of a ton of rubbish after every flight. Every mobile toilet emptier can hold the effluent of two Jumbos. It would take 643 toilet emptiers to pump one Jumbo full of effluent. Me Tarmac, you Jane. Jumbo no fly: Boy lie. 90,000 Jumbos converge on London every day. I could have done the easy thing ...

29 May, 1977

A load of chunk

FRONTING a *World in Action* (Granada) report on the Japanese economy, Mike Scott showed us a Japanese television commercial for one of our most successful exports,

McVitie's Digestive Biscuits, which the Japanese apparently devour in large quantities. Tweedy English actors with hampers and shooting sticks disembarked from a Rolls and set about taking tea alfresco. Tweedy English music occupied the soundtrack, until it was interrupted by an oriental voice deeply whispering the name of the product. 'Macahaviahties Dyahagahestivah Bahiscuhihetah.'

There was some encouragement to be derived from the fact that the Japanese can still occasionally sound awkward trying to be like us. But mostly, as Scott's film reverberantly demonstrated, it's nowadays a case of us sounding awkward trying to be like them. The Japanese economy has us beaten all ends up. Scott stood in front of the Datsun production line, which according to British myth should have been swarming with tiny, snaggle-toothed Japanese workers all sharing the one spanner and toiling 16 hours a day for a bowl of rice. The daunting reality featured a robot welder going about its computerised business while a lone supervisor the size of Rock Hudson looked masterfully on.

Did that mean that the workers replaced by the machine were on the dole? Not at all. The work force is never cut back because the output always goes up. The output will obviously continue to go up as long as other countries do not raise their tariff barriers. Scott neglected to say what would happen if they did, but it wasn't hard to imagine the same production line turning out other things – tanks, for example. It was all very uncomfortable viewing, apart from the solace to be drawn from how funny they sound saying 'McVitie's Digestive Biscuits'.

In *Owner Occupied* (Thames), apparently the pilot show for a new sit-com, Robert Hardy was given another chance to employ the Cherman accent he brought to such perfection when playing Prince Albert in *Edward VII*. This time he was a Cherman officer occupying one of the Channel Islands (I think it must have been Chersey) during World War II. Hannah Gordon was the cuddlesome local beauty who despised everything he stood for. But Hardy was such a luff-able Cherman officer that she plainly found it difficult to resist his charm. That must have been how he got his Iron Cross and wound stripe – charming the Poles to death.

Hannah's father ran the hotel which the Cherman officer had requisitioned as his headquarters. The former was a kind of *Hotel Sahara* with less sand and more ... well, crap, actually. There was a good deal of unchentlemanly behaviour from some of the locals during the Cherman occupation of the Channel Islands. If we see some of that, the series might chust work. Otherwise it will be a load of chunk.

The most solid documentary of the week was *White Rhodesia* (BBC1), presented by Hugh Burnett. He was on screen only two or three times and even when he was there you would have sworn he wasn't. But the people he talked to found themselves spilling all kinds of beans. Gun-toting white ladies might easily have been exploited for satirical mileage. 'I think they'll be frightened to come here. They're awful cowards, those fellows.' Wishful thinking, of course. But it soon became clear that these were brave and even noble people, however misguided. This wasn't satire: it was tragedy.

The best of the whites knew that the blacks who had been loyal to them were in for it. Gently prodded by Burnett, some of them even admitted that if there had been justice in the past, there would be no terror now. One or two were even ready to say that the jig was up. White wisdom had come late, but you could hardly laugh. Their sons are dying one by one and they haven't really got anywhere to go. Imaginative in the scope of its sympathies, this was an outstanding programme.

René Cutforth's trip down memory drain culminated in *The Forties Revisited* (BBC2). Cutforth is that rare thing, a front-man with background. You only have to clock that bashed face to know that here is a man who has lived. His jacket is worn to a frazzle from decades of rubbing shoulders in pubs with the London literary-journalistic-broadcasting intelligentsia. Fitzrovia and Soho weigh heavily on his eye-lids. His voice sounds like tea-chests full of books being shifted about.

Cutforth accompanied his wealth of film clips with some general comments which had substance even when they were sweeping. He took the *Picture Post* view that the nation found itself during the war. Even if you think that it has lost itself again since, this is still probably the most accurate, as well as the most optimistic, interpretation of what happened to Britain in the 1940s. It was a people's war and Cutforth was properly sceptical about the competence and vision with which our rulers fought it. If I can risk a cultural comment of my own, I would like to suggest that here lay the true signi-ficance of Vera Lynn. Hers was the first singing voice that gave no clue to the social class of its owner. It was, and still is, the sound of democracy.

31 July, 1977

Women's lab

AFTER two episodes, *Marie Curie* (BBC2) is clearly estab-lished as an exceptional piece of work. The remaining three episodes can be awaited with confidence as well as impatience.

The series is written by Elaine Morgan, otherwise the co-author, with Brian Gibson, of the remarkable *Joey*, which was repeated last Tuesday night ahead of the second instal-ment of *Marie Curie*, thereby making the evening something of an Elaine Morgan festival. She is a writer who combines sensitivity with analytical power.

It would be easy for any woman writer to wax emotional about Marie Curie, who suffered and died for her science. It must be hard not to claim her achievements as a triumph of her sex, since she was in so many respects the victim of it. But Miss Morgan has resisted this temptation. She has put in all the harsh facts, but has not allowed them to lure her away from the true drama of Marie and Pierre Curie – the idealistic dedication with which he gave his talent to her genius and she gave her genius to the quest for knowledge.

They were a unique couple. Even Hollywood could see that. Casting Greer Garson as Marie and Walter Pidgeon as Pierre, it regaled a less lucky generation than ours with the kind of movie which used to be called a Garson-Pidgeon. Madame was beautiful. Pierre was distinguished. Malnutrition was conveyed with a pretty swoon by Garson, whereupon Pidgeon would look extremely concerned. They held hands as the radium glowed in the dark.

As written by Miss Morgan, produced by Peter Goodchild and directed by John Glenister, the Curie story involves the principal players in a harder brand of graft altogether. Jane Lapotaire plays Marie with no appeal whatsoever to the feminine stereotype. Thin-lipped, washed out and shaking with bottled-up intensity, she looks like tough company. To put it kindly, she lacks small talk. Yet by a remarkable coup on Miss Lapotaire's part, what must have been the beauty of the great scientist's mind is projected with a vividness made all the more intense by the absence of ordinary charm.

In the first episode, science brought Marie and Pierre together. The shy Pierre rhapsodised about the symmetry of crystals. Marie lit up. In the second episode there were hardships. Racked by a baby that would neither sleep nor feed properly, Marie was unable to study. Pierre suggested that she take a year off. It was his solitary moment of male chauvinism. In all other respects their communication was perfect. Nor was it just a matter of him doing what she wanted.

Since theirs was plainly a rapport beyond the ken of ordinary mortals, Miss Morgan has done a good job of putting it within reach of us. There is only the occasional awkward scrap of dialogue to recall the lingering conventions of the Hollywood bio-pic. 'What do you call it?' 'We call it – radioactivity.' Too many such exchanges are still echoing in the moviegoer's mind. 'That's a pretty tune, Glenn. What's it called?' 'Well, it's moonlight outside and it's a sort of serenade ... why don't we call it "Moonlight Serenade"?'

The art direction on the series is highly satisfactory. All the scientific instruments look authentically in period, right down to the innumerable little porcelain dishes in which the salts were refined. In the next episode, if I remember the Curies' biography correctly, eight tons of pitchblende will have to be delivered on the doorstep. Refining a mountain of ore down to a tenth of a gram of radium, Marie lost a stone in weight over four years. It will be interesting to see how Miss Lapotaire manages that. In the end she has to die of leukaemia. But really there was no tragedy – Marie Curie's life was an epic.

The same can't be said about the unwitting heroine of *The Case of Yolande McShane* (Yorkshire). Yolande's mother had not done very much with her life except grow old. Nevertheless it is hard to quarrel with the law of the land, which declares that if people want to go on living nobody should try to stop them. Yolande, however, apparently had other ideas, quietly suggesting to her mother that on the whole it might be more convenient if she knocked herself off. I suppose it happens every day, but what was strange about this particular instance was that the police secured a videotape of the suggestion actually being made. Yolande slipped her mother eighteen Nembutals in a Jelly-tots packet and urged her not to hang about.

As so often happens in these cases, the central issue is less interesting than the fuss made about airing it. There was nothing surprising about Yolande requesting her mother to take the high jump. You didn't have to listen to Yolande for very long before realising that from the moral viewpoint she was no more discriminating than a falling girder. Ethics came into it only when you started considering what the police thought they were up to.

Even here, it seemed to me, we were faced with nothing more sinister than a policeman's desire to play television director. Interviewed about his activities as a television director, he also got a chance to play television star. He must have thought all his Christmases were coming at once. If Yolande's mother had actually swallowed the barbiturates he would have got the chance to play Dr Kildare. You can bet that he would have jumped at it. As for Yorkshire Television's large talk about the public's right to know, it is hooey. They just had a red-hot stretch of tape showing some bitch talking her mother into snuffing herself. One way or another they had to get it on the air.

In *Portrait* (BBC2) Peter Blake spent several days attempting to capture Twiggy's likeness. He failed miserably. While creation was in progress, artist and model reminisced about the allegedly golden 1960s. 'It was like a complete Renaissance event,' opined Peter. 'Yeah, that was it,' concurred Twiggy. 'It was just like a Renaissance.' Except that in the Renaissance the artists knew how to draw.

28 August, 1977

Bonjour twistesse

THE Beeb having fielded a reasonably adequate substitute for *The Brothers* – I refer, of course, to *Rough Justice* (BBC1) – the pressure on ITV was redoubled to come up with a reasonably adequate substitute for their own all-time hit sudser, the one and only *Bouquet of Barbed Wire*. Clearly an impossible task, yet with *The Foundation* (ATV) they have done something to accomplish it. The first series finished on Friday, but you can be certain that it won't be the last.

Sensibly there has been no attempt to recapture the basic *Bouquet* gimmick, by which every character concerned went to bed with all the others, so that you ended up with a genteel version of those Marquis de Sade fantasies in which the butcher, the baker and the candlestick maker find themselves being roped into the action. The *Foundation* plot is more of a reversion to the trusty *Planemakers* format. Big business, rich living, tough at the top, etc. The decision-makers, etc.

For some reason, even though the Beeb is constantly attempting versions of its own, this format flourishes best on ITV. The only time the Corporation ever got it right was with *The Brothers*, and there they cheated by transposing the idea downwards, so that the high-flying executives looked and sounded lower middle class, or even plebeian. *The Foundation* is the format in its pure state, with all the principal characters placed firmly in the equestrian order or above. Apart from a token brace of lovable proles who seem to have been included mainly so that their up-market acquaintances can gain some ethical credit by being nice to them, the only unusual element in the set-up is that the decision-maker furthest to the forefront is wearing skirts instead of trousers.

Davinia Prince, played by Lynette Davies, is a businesswoman of flair and determination. But her tremulous lower lip, which under the stress of emotion droops to reveal a glistening row of tiny teeth, is the clue to her susceptible heart. Against her better judgment, she is in love with a married man, a foreign wheeler-dealer called Philippe, pronounced Philippe. 'Do you know how you make me feel, Philippe?' she muses as they lie together in her luxurious bed with only their heads sticking out. 'I theenk so. You make me feel the same way.'

Philippe likes making love with the light on, a sure sign of Continental sophistication. In fact he is so sophisticated that he is sometimes hard for the ordinary viewer to understand. 'Do you know the French word, twist?' I didn't, but realised on reflection that he meant the French word *triste*.

Davinia and Philippe ought to be eternal lovers, but are doomed by circumstances to a fleeting affair. It is inevitable that they should feel twist. To match her slightly atavistic, early 1950s grooming (think of Ann Todd in *The Sound Barrier* and you've got it exactly), Davinia discreetly flaunts a Rank-starlet version of patrician elocution. Not even her passion for Philippe can put a dent in her refinement. 'Ay can't control it,' she whimpers. 'The trouble with being in love is all you do is feel, feel, feel!'

Lest Davinia fly too high for the rest of us to identify with her, she is provided with a sister, Katherine. Straightforward, no-nonsense, unstuffy Katherine. Katherine the school-teacher. It might be a private school, but still we can see that Katherine's origins are nothing grand. It follows that Davinia's aren't either. Although she might now be up there with Them, nevertheless she started off down here with Us. And while Katherine might not have Davinia's privileges, she hasn't got her problems either. 'Do be careful,' Katherine staunchly advises her beautiful sister. 'Try not to get yourself hurt.' Davinia is lucky to have so wise a confidante as Katherine. After all, Katherine's advice might easily have been the opposite. 'Do be careless. Try to bugger yourself up as much as possible.'

There is no secret about why soap operas make compulsive television. They simplify life. It is not so much a matter of simplifying events as of simplifying character. Most of the events in *The Foundation* could easily happen in real life – Davinias are continually fighting their way up from nowhere for the privilege of falling into bed with Philippe and feeling twist. But in real life the matter of character is never so ele-mentary. In a soap opera, character is destiny: everything anybody does is determined by his nature. In real life we are stuck with the existentialist responsibility of remaking ourselves every morning. It is we who are the real decision-makers. By the time Friday rolls around we are worn out from taking the rap. Hence the charm of being able to reach out and switch on Davinia, who is always and only what she is.

4 September, 1977

Heaven help we

A GUEST of *Parkinson* (BBC1), Cliff Richard sang a song of his own composition. 'There's nothing left between we two,' he warbled thinly. Us were in luck.

Writing, Cliff told his host, was important to him. 'Why hasn't that special woman entered your life?' asked the puzzled Parky. Cliff said, as he has been saying for the past twelve years, that there was no point in getting married just for the sake of it. His argument gained force from the consideration that a decade or so of celibacy can do wonders for the creative powers. Vital, ageless, and now an important writer, Cliff is a shining example to all of we.

World About Us (BBC2) did a tropical jungle number. Emphasis was on the delicately worked out logic underlying the lush biosystem. Nevertheless the script had to admit that the untrained eye might find some of the life-forms hard to take. 'There *are* horrors here,' the voice-over admitted grudgingly. In triumphant proof, a spider the size and shape of a roller-skate in a mink coat came charging at the camera. A battalion of army ants discovered a beetle in their path. They converged on it. Instead of a beetle, there was a beetle-shaped pile of army ants.

The scrum broke up and the ants moved on, several of them carrying recognisable beetle-components. Otherwise there was nothing to mark the spot of the beetle's lonely

death. Are its wife and children still keeping a vigil at the
door of the dung-hill? And what degree of moral temptation
are the programme-makers faced with? Do they set up their
cameras and wait patiently until the army ants happen to
encounter a beetle, or do they just sort of nudge – well, not
even nudge, really: more like, you know, *help* – a beetle into
the right spot? All of these are among the eternal mysteries.

But if Nature is strange, God, its creator, is even stranger.
In *The Long Search* (BBC2) Ronald Eyre is engaged in a big-
budget quest for the ultimate secrets of religious belief. In
the annals of the channels, there has never been a tougher
battle than the one between this series and Bamber Gas-
coigne's *The Christians*, still running on ITV. Bamber has the
advantage of focus – he deals with one faith. Ronald, dealing
in all faiths, has the advantage of range. The first episode
went to India: Ganges, garbage, stuff like that. 'I was starting to pick up clues.' The second went to Indianapolis,
where there are 1,100 Protestant churches. The third episode
… but there is no point in trying to prove to you that I have
been keeping up. Immunised from birth against religion of
any kind, your critic can only look on longingly. The photo-
graphy is very nice.

Faith breeds courage, however. In a characteristically
adventurous *Everyman* (BBC1), Soviet persecution of religion
was laid bare. It needed laying bare, because for some reason
there are a lot of people – not just Communists – who are
intent on covering it up. What? Persecution in Russia *nowadays*? And they smile at you tolerantly. Yet the facts say that
it still goes on, making new martyrs every year.

At least there are no longer any tolerant smiles when you
suggest that the South African Government is defeating its
own ends. Even an idiot can see that all you accomplish by
killing a man like Steve Biko is to ensure that insurrection,
when it comes, will be led by fanatics instead of moderates.
World in Action (Granada) went in and dug: a good, brave job.

Biko's friends spoke with great dignity. His wife would

have been less heart-breaking if she had not maintained her composure so well: you tremble for what must surely happen to anyone so noble, when nobility is the very thing the desperate oppressor is determined to expunge. Biko wanted a multi-racial society. His successors are unlikely to be so tolerant. The police who killed him might as well have strangled their own children with their bare hands.

Back in the world of comedy, the *Labour Party Conference* (BBC2 and ITV) was rich fare for anyone with an afternoon to kill. Barely articulate delegates demanded that educational admissions criteria should be relaxed for disadvantaged groups. Scorn was allayed somewhat by the fact that the same sort of people, some of them even less articulate, argued for a course of action that really *would* help – i.e., more nursery schools.

It was sad, though, to see that in Britain it should still be necessary for people to go on asking for so indispensable a thing. But any inclinations to gloom were instantly dispelled when the director cut to shots of Callaghan and/or Foot miming concern and/or keenness in the background. Joan Lestor was a splendid chairperson. When a speaker's time was up, she slung him off the platform. 'Thanks, comrade. Lovely speech. Don't spoil it.' And back the poor sod went for another year of anonymous toil.

9 October, 1977

Nershment

A T least once a year, *Horizon* (BBC2) tells you to watch out for the sun. Last year it wasn't producing enough neutrinos. This year it's getting hotter. Even in cool countries like Britain, rays from space heat up the foreheads of television executives, causing them to run amok and purchase rotten American series about mechanical women or men with supernormal powers.

The latest man with supernormal powers is *Man From Atlantis* (LWT), who can breathe underwater. At the start of each episode, younger viewers are warned not to copy his trick of sleeping in a full bath-tub, but they are not warned against copying his acting. Man from Atlantis – or Mark Harris, as he is known to his human friends – wears dark glasses when he walks among us. Yet Mark's elevated dialogue is unmistakable evidence of alien origin: like all the supernormal heroes in the Hollywood serials of old, he has been unable to master the apostrophe. 'Do not follow me,' he tells the beautiful scientist, 'I am going to the main airlock.' When he doesn't know, he says, 'I do not know.' If he knows, he says, 'I will tell you later.'

But a man who has to hold his breath all the time can be forgiven for stilted diction. Back in the water, Mark can flood his gills and relax. Now we can see the way they must have looked in Atlantis, with their webbed hands and long yellow bathing trunks. Meanwhile, alien water-breathing parasites invade from space. They adopt human form but we can tell they are extraterrestrials by their unblinking gaze and their habit of saying, 'I need nershment,' when they want to eat.

Only Mark can stop them. The beautiful scientist gazes at him with an unspoken love. Have she and Mark been climbing into the bath together? Or is their union an anatomical impossibility? What goes on under the yellow bathing trunks? Perhaps he is webbed there too.

Although there can be no possible doubt that shows like *Man From Atlantis* liquefy the cerebral cortex, it remains a moot point whether TV violence can warp the personality. Milton Shulman has watched television for years, yet shows no signs of becoming an axe-murderer. The topic has been aired all over again recently by the trial of Ronny Zamora, some of which we saw on *Tonight* (BBC1).

After watching thousands of people being killed on television, Ronny started killing people on his own account. To the anti-TV-violence lobby it must look an open and shut case. There is, however, an additional factor, namely Ronny's stepfather, who according to Ronny's mother has made a regular practice of beating Ronny up. This would be a more plausible reason for Ronny's psychopathic behaviour, but harder to prate about. It's easier to rail against *Starsky and Hutch* than to deal with the likelihood that a lot of parents are actively engaged in turning their children into killers.

The best reason for objecting to the number of imported American TV series is that so many of them are no good. Most of the fuzz operas, for example, have nothing in them except the weekly car-chase. Nobody would really miss *Cannon* or *Dan August* or *The Streets of San Francisco*. Even here, though, the matter is really not all that simple. I wouldn't want to lose *The Rockford Files* (BBC1); James Garner, a droll leading man during his time in the movies, is worth watching even when the script is routine. There is also the consideration that clearing the screen of derivative American series might do nothing but make room for derivative series of our own. Look, or rather don't look, at *1990* (BBC2), the *n*th series about Britain's totalitarian future, which will apparently consist of Barbara Kellermann standing haughtily around while Edward Woodward and other luckless males try to stop the script from reaching her.

Many harsh things have been said in this column about Ron Pickering, but he did a good job of fronting a *World About Us* (BBC2) on Cuban sport. The Cubans obviously enjoy the whole idea of sporting excellence, perhaps because they live in such a favourable climate. Selective schools train the future champions, but nobody calls it elitism. Pretty girls are encouraged to look on while young boxers clobber each other, but nobody calls it sexism. The Revolution reigns supreme, but nobody calls it totalitarianism. Everybody is running and jumping happily, but you couldn't help wondering what would happen to anyone who wanted to stand still.

Sight and Sound in Concert (BBC2 and Radio 4) was a simul-cast starring Elkie Brooks, an ex-scruff turned glamour-queen. Along with the well-cut clothes comes some Helen Reddy-type show-biz patter ('Whew! I'm hot,') but at least she has not yet succumbed to making shapes with her mouth. The two Abba girls, featured in *The Best of Abba* (BBC1), make shapes constantly. So does *David Essex* (BBC1), in addition to wobbling his lower jaw sideways. But the most dedicated mouth-shaper of the lot is non-singer *Pam Ayres* (LWT), who can smile a map of Australia.

On *Nationwide* (BBC1) the lovely Sue Lawley played host to French lingerie expertette Nadine Grimaud. French models paraded in dreamy nightwear. 'Ziss one is so sexee,' purred Nadine, and she was right. 'My goodness,' cried the worried Sue, 'it's probably very uncomfortable in bed.'

Unabashed, the girls continued to sway past, each of them accompanied by a descriptive comment from Nadine. 'Ziss one is also veree sexee ... sportive ... sexee.' As Sue was patently aware, it was an arousing display. Randy camera-men zoomed and focused desperately on filmy knickers hugging soft crotches. For any watching rapists, it must have got the evening off to a flying start.

16 October, 1977

A boy forever

MAGNUS MAGNUSSON misquoted Keats on *Mastermind* (BBC1). 'A thing of beauty,' he informed us, 'is a boy forever.' For a moment you got a picture of him as a Roman poet in a low-cut toga, with vine leaves in his hair.

But the picture was all in the mind. On the screen he was still Magnus the Icelandic inquisitor. He was lucky to be on screen at all. The Beeb's technicians pulled the plugs on the Queen. They even pulled the plugs on Angela Rippon, which is going a bit far. Thursday night's nine o'clock *News* (BBC1) was an abridged version, with Angie given barely enough time to breathe hello. The vacant running-time was made up with old Interlude featurettes from the 1950s, including the one where a disembodied hand makes a clay pot.

Not having been raised in Britain, I had never seen this most famous of all television creations. Viewed even once, it was hypnotically boring. Viewed time after time over a span of years, it must have worked like a mantra – you could do transcendental meditation to it, or perhaps even levitate. I had never realised that the pot was doomed to remain unfinished: forever changing shape, it goes everywhere and nowhere, like the history of the human race.

Or like *Charlie's Angels* (Thames), which has succeeded in uniting the population of the world like nothing since the common cold. Half-wits of more than a hundred nations watch every episode. In the latest series there has been a slight change of cast. Farrah Fawcett-Majors, for some reason the most popular of the original Angels, has been replaced by Cheryl Ladd. Cheryl's teeth are big and strong like Farrah's so she will probably become equally famous, if my theory is correct. (My theory is that the majority of males in the audience harbour an unspoken desire to be eaten alive.)

Since Farrah is now a millionairess, which is a large reward for doing almost nothing except look healthy, it is perhaps permissible to say that she had a bad case of duck's disease, to the point where the directors had to be careful in the long shots. Cheryl's behind is a lot further from the ground.

Anyway, Cheryl, or Chris as she is called in the series, now joins Jaclyn, known as Kelly, and Kate, who plays the taxing role of Sabrina. Commanded by Charlie's ghostly voice, each week they leap pertly into action against relays of dumb but sinister heavies. It's a sort of George Plimpton number, whereby the Angels solve the crime by merging unobtrusively into the milieu.

If the offence is perpetrated in Hawaii, they immediately become surfers. If it happens in an ice show they are transformed into ice skaters. They are equally ready to impersonate nuclear physicists, test pilots and sword swallowers. One of the two big questions in the viewer's mind is why the heavies are always so slow to catch on. The other big question, of course, concerns the Angels' love life. Is Charlie getting them all?

'Dickens did not write what the people wanted,' said Chesterton. 'He wanted what the people wanted.' Leaving aside the awkward fact that there is undoubtedly a sense in which the people want *Charlie's Angels*, Chesterton was stating a great truth. Dickens did not talk down. He was genuine in everything, even his sentimentality, which was really just a powerful assertion that people could be noble beyond their circumstances – an assertion he had a right to make, since he had the courage to see circumstances for what they were, and the optimistic energy to set about getting them changed. *Hard Times* (Granada) continues to be remarkably successful in transmitting the largeness of his spirit.

Dickens knows, and lets you know he knows, that he is writing melodrama: one of the functions of his style performs is to win your consent while he simplifies. It follows that a dramatisation must find a style to match, and here it has happened. We can see that the relationship between Gradgrind and Louisa is overdrawn, but we don't mind, because the high emphasis is subtly handled, so that you get intensity rather than crassness. What Dickens spells out is made to seem natural.

Jacqueline Tong does very well as Louisa. The line about the chimneys spitting fire at night was not shirked: she looked ready for arousal, even if the arouser had to be the detested Bounderby. Now Harthouse is on the scene, in the person of Edward Fox, here licensed to employ his full range of gentlemanly effects. He gives it the voice. ('Vair lawdble' means 'Very laudable'.) He gives it the raised eyebrow. In short, he gives it the works. You could have roasted a turkey in the glances exchanged between Harthouse and Louisa.

In *You Never Can Tell* (BBC1), first in a new series of *Play of the Month*, there was a similarly high charge circulating between Kika Markham (Gloria) and Robert Powell (Valentine). Here was ample proof that Shaw knew a thing or two about desire. He may have been beyond sex himself – or beneath it or above it, depending on your viewpoint – but he could see something of what it did to other people. Even in this, a play pleasant, the emotions can be made as fierce as the actors are able to manage. Shaw knew that love is real, and hurts. He just took a light tone.

So did the director, James Cellan Jones, and with excellent results. Apart from Dolly, an impossible role with which there is nothing to be done except play against the text, the personnel were satisfactory throughout. The cast was so strong that Cyril Cusack was playing the waiter.

As for Kika Markham, I had better rein myself in, except to say that if she ever grows tired of trying to change the world with her political activities, she has an excellent chance of changing it as an actress. She has a marvellous gift. The boom operator was almost equally forthcoming. At one point he laid the shadow of the microphone across Cyril Cusack's forehead with such precision that you could practically read the brand-name.

6 November, 1977

Chastity pants

TELEVISION cameras were absent from the two most sensational news stories of the year, thereby disproving the hallowed theory that every event is a media event or else nothing.

84

There were no cameras watching when the German commandos triumphantly stormed the hijacked airliner in Somalia. News programmes had to make do with the same sort of Artist's Impressions which appeared in the daily papers. Nor was there even a single lens present at the even more epoch-making moment when Mormon missionary Kirk Anderson succumbed to the blandishments of former beauty queen Joyce McKinney. Whatever took place, took place away from prying eyes. Yet the world is fascinated.

Fascinated above all by Kirk's underpants. It appears that Mormon missionaries wear a special nether garment which renders it easier for them to remain pure when facing up to operational hazards in the field. Whether the chastity pants help ward off temptation, or else make temptation impossible to act upon once yielded to, or both, remains unclear. News reporters on all channels gave details of what was happening in court, but the chastity pants, if mentioned, were not described. Surely I was not alone in wondering how these nullifying knickers worked their trick.

Roughing out a few speculative designs in my notebook, I quickly realised that the garment, like a multi-role combat aircraft, would have to fulfil varying, and in some cases directly contrary, functions. It would be impossible to eliminate body wastes, for example, without exposing the potentially unruly member to the outside atmosphere. Once released, the aforesaid appendage could obviously get up to anything, unless artificially restricted. Some form of clamp was indicated. But in that case ...

By this time my sketch looked like a cross between a tank turret and a lagged boiler, so I gave up. Television news programmes will come of age when we are told these things as a matter of course, and are not left in a fever of curiosity.

Rock Follies of 77 (Thames) came to the end of its exultant course. In the last two episodes the Little Ladies were embroiled in various processes of paying dues, going through changes, and getting it together. Actually the only thing that occurred was the inevitable: an unwritten law, that talent is destiny, was working itself out. Anna and Q went to the wall. Dee and Rox headed for the top.

The chief subject of Howard Schuman's continuously excellent script was how the remorseless logic of showbiz success is really both those things – remorseless and logical. In real life there might be room for sentiment, but in the sentimental world of popular music everything is real.

Even at their most imaginative, all the details were authentic. Kitty Schreiber (Beth Porter) really *would* say, 'We don't want to flaunt our dirty linen in front of the *Melody Maker*,' and the *Melody Maker* reporter really *would* shamble about making semi-articulate sounds. Close observation was the basis of the show's inventiveness. *Rock Follies* had its low moments, but on the whole it deserves its reputation as one of the most original television series ever made. And on top of all that, it had Little Nell.

Rock Follies Explored, as they say, the Medium, but Exploring the Medium was not its first concern. Its first concern was to tell a story. Any work of art which sets out in the first instance to Explore its Medium will never be any good. This ancient truth sorely needs to be restated in a week which saw Verdi's *Macbeth* (BBC2) given a production whose transcendental lousiness was rubbed in by a swathe of *Radio Times* articles hailing it as a breakthrough. These strident claims – several of which were made by the producer, Brian Large, on his own behalf – added up to a confident assertion that the opera had at last been translated into television terms. In fact it had been translated into a disaster. It sounded all right, but it looked like hell.

Calling it 'the first British television studio production' helped distract attention from the awkward fact that within living memory Southern TV transmitted the Glyndebourne *Macbeth* with brilliant success. I suppose Brian Large would have called that transmission stage-bound, but since it was a superlative staging anyway, and was shot with great subtlety, there was small reason to object. Besides, even if it is granted that an opera needs to be translated into television terms, Brian Large is not necessarily the ideal man for the task. Some of the more gullible critics might have cried up his production of *The Flying Dutchman* ('made television history' – *TV Times*), but in fact it was a load of old rubbish compared with, say, the recent German television production of *Fidelio*, which really *did* exploit the flexibility of the camera, although with such delicacy that you hardly noticed.

There was no hope of failing to notice what Brian Large got up to with 'Macbeth.' The settings and costumes recalled the Orson Welles film of the same name, a cheap rush-job which in turn recalled Eisenstein. The designer informed us, *per media* the *TV Times*, that he was 'not too worried' about where the action was supposed to be taking place and that he was bent on achieving a 'Slavonic feel', thereby avoiding the 'Dark Ages thing'.

I can refer him with confidence to Verdi's letters, where he will find the composer always careful to remind ambitious designers that the action is set in Scotland, not in Ancient Rome, and that they should therefore confine themselves to achieving a Scottish feel. The Dark Ages thing was exactly what he was after.

The banquet scene was set in a cross between an automat and a launderette, with a plastic pig rotating on a spit. Containing some of Verdi's finest early music, this is a hard scene to muck up, but here was proof that it can be done. The final battle was feeble beyond belief. Banquo's ghost (Verdi was particularly concerned that the Brian Larges of his day should not fart around with Banquo's ghost) turned up as a head on a platter – suddenly it's *Salome*! What Macbeth was doing with a Star of David scratched on his chest I hesitate to think. But enough.

The second part of *Eustace and Hilda* (BBC2), adapted by Alan Seymour from L. P. Hartley, had excellent performances in the name parts. Christopher Strauli was so vulnerable, wet and exhausted you could hardly stand him, whereas Susan Fleetwood was vitality incarnate. She has the air of resembling what the Winged Victory of Samothrace might have looked like if only it had kept its head.

20 November, 1977

Olde rubbishe

A SSIGNED to exhilarate us during the Festive Season were a host of British and American entertainers. It was easy to tell the British from the Americans. The British were mainly in drag, whereas the Americans were either very old or dead.

The star of *Bing Crosby's Merrie Olde Christmas* (ATV) lived a long time, but not quite long enough to find out how his last big spectacular was received. Through no fault of Bing's, the show turned out to be a load of olde rubbishe. Some of the jokes were aimed at America, thereby tipping Lord Grade's pudgy hand: once again he was hoping to score a hit in two separate markets.

The setting was a country house right-here-in Britain, with Bing's semi-talented family playing the guests and Stanley Baxter playing most of the servants, these latter being based on characters in *Upstairs, Downstairs*, a series much beloved in America. What the Americans made of Baxter in drag it is hard to guess, but from where I sat his act was just another dud ingredient in the general sludge. Bing looked as tired as the gags. There was a song about 'geneology' – by which, presumably, 'genealogy' was meant.

Perry Como's Olde Englishe Christmas (BBC2) was similarly guaranteed to leave you colde. If the show had been called 'Perry Como's Olde Italiane Christmas' it would have made more sense, since Perry's origins, though European, tend more towards the Mediterranean. But for reasons unknown the chosen setting was a country house, situated right-here-in Britain.

An ice rink was laid down over the lawn so that John Curry, a dream in rose pink, might skate a frozen solo. Petula Clark, dripping with sequins, sang a number containing such exhortations as 'Hold on, baby, to this beautiful thing.' Perry gave his usual impersonation of a man who has been simultaneously told to say 'Cheese' and shot in the back with a poisoned arrow.

But at least the Americans, however advanced in life's course, were determined to retain their trousers. The British were equally bent – the word seems not misplaced – on losing theirs. As always, nobody was quicker at climbing into high heels than Dick Emery, star of *The Dick Emery Christmas Show* (BBC1), an extravaganza which left you wondering whether it wasn't time to abolish Christmas entirely. The setting was a British country house. There was a mystery afoot. The plot was meant to confuse, although in the event nothing was more confusing than the way dire jokes were swamped with ecstatic audience reaction.

Most of Emery's alleged humour was about poo, pee and buggery. 'Peter, I want to have a peep at Uranus.' 'Surely you want a telescope for that.' 'I want to have a look at Mars as well.' Somewhere on the sound-track, a lady died laughing at that one. But not even her expiring cries would have stood out in the general uproar of hilarity which greeted Emery's every appearance in female costume. He had only to pull on the wig, paint the lips, wriggle into the frock and hop up on the heels. The result was panic.

On ITV, neither Stanley Baxter nor Benny Hill had a new show to offer this year. They gave us 'best ofs' instead. *The Best of Benny Hill* (Thames) showed no more signs than usual of being significantly different from the worst. The trailer was all I could stand. From Stanley Baxter we expect something more adventurous, but *The Best of Stanley Baxter* (LWT) unintentionally reinforced the impression that he is happiest as a female impersonator. Nor does he seem particularly concerned about which female he impersonates, as long as the costume gives him a chance to show off his legs. These are long, smooth and finely turned, but the hips at the top of them are irredeemably masculine. There is something desperate about his mimicry of female movements. He is too good at it: the laughter dies, leaving a sad admiration.

The Two Ronnies (BBC1) tried hard. Apart from the regular Piggy Malone number – which never works, but gives the boys a chance to grope a scantily clad damsel – the show was reasonably diverting, and for a wonder it was not until the last item that the stars appeared in female attire. The idea of either Ronnie, but especially the large one, coming on in drag is meant to be automatically amusing because of the otherwise heavy emphasis on heterosexuality. But if it strikes you that all the stridently proclaimed interest in tit and bum is pretty hysterical anyway, then the frocks look unsurprising rather than otherwise. Like most British comedians, the Ronnies operate in a unisex limbo: theirs is the straight version, but it is just as camp as the bent one.

The hero of *Mike Yarwood's Christmas Show* (BBC1) is a remarkable impersonator for more reasons than mere talent. Far from being happy in drag, he does his best to avoid it – to the extent that he would rather farm out the job of aping Margaret Thatcher than attempt it himself. Perhaps I am making butch claims on my own account, but I'm bound to say it's a relief to know that at least one comedian isn't aching to get into his beads.

'The best fun is on ITV,' squeaked the *TV Times*. Adduced as evidence for this assertion was *Max's Holiday Hour* (Thames), starring Max Bygraves. Max's show was variously billed as 'a fun-packed hour of Christmas entertainment' and 'a whole lot of festive fun'. It was no more fun than a sinus wash, but on the other hand it was no less fun either, and there is never any telling what will make the watching millions laugh.

They had some cause to laugh at *Morecambe and Wise* (BBC1), whose Christmas special stuck to their by-now-classic format, including a production number sung and danced by a host of the Beeb's familiar faces. To the strains of 'Nothing Like a Dame' the likes of Barry Norman were allowed to fulfil their fantasies by dancing in sailor suits. This made me very envious of the likes of Barry Norman.

Penelope Keith was the guest. Eddie Braben's script invited her to mistake Ernie for Kermit the Frog. Angie Rippon danced through. Every component of the show was triple-tested. The sense of adventure was consequently lacking. Eric was twice as funny busking with Dickie Davies on ITV's *World of Sport* on Christmas Eve.

Getting down to the dregs, *The Little and Largest Show on Earth* (BBC1) showed the inevitable effect of straining a comic turn beyond its natural capacity – the two lads ended up as guests on their own show. Little and Large have one trick, which they work to death. Little tries to sing a song while Large keeps interrupting him with impersonations. Large is a gifted impersonator, but Little's lack of inspiration is scarcely ameliorated by making a point of it. Little is not pretending to be just standing there. He is just standing there. Meanwhile Large knocks himself out. There is a certain terrible fascination to it, like watching two men share one parachute.

But better an eternity in Hell with Little, Large and Max Bygraves than a single *Christmas with the Osmonds* (BBC1). Generations of Osmonds gathered on the snowy heights of Provost, Utah, where they set about the task of conveying their good cheer. Their good cheer is awful because you know they are never not like that. The Osmonds are not even phoney: they are sincerely vacuous. 'Our special friend Andy Williams' was the guest star. It is a damning thing to say, but he fitted in perfectly. Little Jimmy Osmond was present.

Nowadays little Jimmy is not so little, but he is still incontestably the Bad Sight of any week he might happen to turn up in.

Karen Kain, a Kanadian – sorry, Canadian – ballerina featured in *The Lively Arts* (BBC2), was the thing I liked best about Christmas. Watching her dance, you could forget the world without feeling that you were running away. But otherwise television, especially when it was trying to be funny, offered little escape from the realities of a mean age. Eliot has a line somewhere about the laceration of laughter at what ceases to amuse.

1 January, 1978

Doors

No use denying that *Washington: Behind Closed Doors* (BBC1) is gripping stuff. It gets into your mind like Cow Gum: tacky but inexorable.

Doors, as it is called in the trade, had its origins in the mighty intellect of John Ehrlichman, who you will remember was once a Nixon aide chiefly distinguishable by his fanatical loyalty. After being indicted and locked up he became chiefly distinguishable by his fanatical disloyalty, but there is nothing remarkable in that, since the abiding characteristic in men like Ehrlichman is not loyalty but fanaticism. He wrote a novel, which forms the basis for the series, which unsurprisingly neglects to feature any character easily recognisable as Ehrlichman.

You would have thought that Nixon had dragged the Bill of Rights through the mud without Ehrlichman's assistance. The series does, however, feature a character based on Ehrlichman's equally charming colleague Haldeman. Played with chilling authenticity by Robert Vaughn, he goes under the name of Frank Flaherty, but we would do best to think of him as Haldeman and Ehrlichman rolled into one. Any portrait of Haldeman is a portrait of Ehrlichman, especially when Ehrlichman is the one painting it. How can Tweedledum tell you about Tweedledee without telling you about himself?

Anyway, by the time it has been expanded into a TV series Ehrlichman's vision, no longer under its author's control, has stopped being one man's cheap novel and started being a whole generation's big-budget parable. It is by fictions that the facts are remembered if they are to be remembered at all, and the first thing to say about *Doors* is that it is not entirely to be despised. Like *Roots* it has its naiveties, but once again they spring less from cynicism than simplicity of heart. The main effort goes into driving home the lesson, and it seems to at least one viewer that they've got at least half the lesson right — not a bad proportion, as historical lessons go.

Nixon was out to subvert the Constitution of the United States. In *Doors* Richard Monckton, the Nixon figure, is shown doing the same thing. Actually the series is often kinder to Nixon than the facts warrant, since it shows his abuse of power springing more from faults of character than from the will, when there is good evidence that Nixon didn't just drift into subversion but headed straight for it from an early date. But even though the script leaves his motives blurred, nevertheless it does make clear that Nixon was in the process of forming, and ruling by, a Presidential Party — the very thing which the Founding Fathers were determined to prevent. The Nixon administration was deplorable not so much for its incidental crimes, which have been committed by every other administration as well, but for its central impulse. This is a difficult message to get hold of and transmit, but *Doors* has managed it and therefore deserves praise.

With the main idea so robustly put, it doesn't matter so much that a lot of the detail is weak. Besides, the leading roles are in some cases more powerfully cast than the script deserves, thereby providing that feeling of solidity which often goes to make strong soap opera more memorable than weak art. Jason Robards has tricked out the character of Monckton with every nervous spasm and paranoiac twitch that ever racked Nixon's chaotic body.

Some of the best scenes are shot mainly from behind, to show Monckton/Nixon feeling up an acquaintance. The arm is placed with would-be confidence around the victim's shoulder. Then the hand attached to the arm becomes unsure of itself and starts shifting position. Robards has even succeeded in echoing Nixon's unique slouching walk, with the arms out of coordination with the legs – a physical reflection of the recriminative battle being waged in his spirit.

And so on down the line of leading characters, with Cliff Robertson in poised command as CIA boss William Martin, a role presumably based on Richard Helms. Martin is a heavily idealised personification of what the CIA was actually up to throughout that period, but there does happen to be a tinge of justification for making him a good guy. (And by handing the character to Robertson, of course, you make him a good guy automatically.) Nixon did, after all, favour the FBI, traditionally the intelligence agency most concerned with making sure that the State kept track of its enemies at home. The CIA was more concerned with enemies abroad.

The series takes it for granted that the CIA was justified in committing assassination, in order to avert World War III. In fact such activities practically guarantee the loss of World War III by handing the moral advantage to the other side, but this is plainly too awkward a subject for the scriptwriters to tackle. A forgivable omission, but unfortunately it leaves them with little to say about Kissinger, who in the series is called Carl Tessler and does nothing more reprehensible than manifest a taste for power. The missing half of the lesson starts, or ought to start but doesn't, with him. My personal choice of villain in the Nixon years is Kissinger, since he was bright enough to know that in contriving with the President to hide his foreign policy from Congress he was subverting the Constitution.

More of that at a later date, however: the series might yet reach such conclusions, or others I haven't thought of. At the moment it is enough to know that the USA can turn out, for popular consumption, a TV show which faces the fact that its Government can be headed by somebody who doesn't know the difference between right and wrong and that there will be clever men, who do know the difference, keen and even desperate to serve him. You can't imagine the Soviet Union coming clean in the same fashion, although I suppose a series called *Kremlin: Behind High Walls* could be based on Krushchev's speech to the Twentieth Party Congress in 1956, if Krushchev himself were not now out of favour.

8 January, 1978

Melly's golden stream

IN *Arena* (BBC2) we got a chance to watch George Melly having a pee. He didn't set the Thames on fire, but if the Thames had been on fire he might well have put it out. He was standing there a long time – talking as well, of course.

The subject of Melly's spiel was Surrealism. Melly knows a lot about the British branch of this artistic movement, since he used to hob-nob with its founder members. Clad in leather hat and ankle-length leather coat, he squatly revisited the old haunts, telling stories of yestere'en. Students of Melly would have heard it all before, but it was still richly aromatic stuff. Reminiscence poured out of him in a golden stream. As an introduction to the current Surrealism retrospective at the Hayward Gallery the item more than served the turn.

The same subject received less engaging treatment in the first episode of *The South Bank Show* (LWT), starring Melvyn Bragg. Beautiful in a new three-piece suit, Melvyn vowed that his new programme would bring us 'both the latest and the best in the arts of our times'. A mind-boggling scope was evoked. 'We'll be filming Ted Hughes's latest poem and Ken Dodd's latest performance.' There would be romance: the audience would be wafted 'to Abu Dhabi with Edna O'Brien'. Lost in the dunes with the gorgeous green-eyed colleen and her smoky voice! If this was the arts, where had they been keeping the stuff all this time?

Melvyn's guest critics were fully up to the standards of glamour established by his prospectus. Germaine Greer had her hair in a frizz and Gerald Scarfe sported a blue open-neck Yves St Laurent shirt exactly matching his eyes. A touch of make-up ensured that his expanse of bare chest did not flare for the camera.

They all looked terrific. Unfortunately they didn't sound that way. Not a lot got *said*. Even old Germs was strangely muted. Melvyn introduced the forthcoming *Julia* as an important event, perhaps even the film of 1978. Having by chance already seen this movie and been struck by its essential bogusness, I was expecting Germaine to be scathing, but instead she showed clear signs of having been affected by Melvyn's diffident vocabulary. Gerald, on the other hand, didn't think much of the movie, but somehow lacked the words to tell us why.

Neither Germs nor Gerald seemed particularly crazy about *Flint*, the David Mercer play due to appear the following night on BBC1. Melvyn hastened to assure us that the play was a worthy effort, whatever its flaws. You got the sense that he had one eye on how the Beeb might react to having a play slagged before it went out. The first half of the show closed with a desultory item about Surrealism. With George Melly micturating on a rival channel, Melvyn had to find another way of enlivening the discussion. While

Germs and Gerald traded damp observations, three models stood about in the background with Surrealist things on their heads.

So far, so blah — but the second half saved the night. Melvyn interviewed Paul McCartney, who was even more engaging than you might expect. The item was a naked appeal for a wide audience, but there is no point in begrudging Melvyn his populist tendencies. Nor was he necessarily aiming at the lowest common denominator. More like the highest common factor: anyone seriously interested in music would have been glad to hear what McCartney had to say, although it might have been better had he said a bit more. But McCartney's contribution guaranteed the show's future success, and I for one will be tuning in, if only for the romance. To Abu Dhabi with Edna O'Brien! To Ultima Thule with Margaret Drabble! To the Vatican with Marina Warner!

Stunned by its own publicity, Granada's *Laurence Olivier Presents* series was slow to find its feet, but its final presentations were must viewing, if you don't count *Come Back, Little Sheba*. The latest and last offering was *Daphne Laureola*, by James Bridie. A hit in 1949, the play has not been much thought of since, but on this evidence it is a crafty text by a playwright whose reputation should never have been allowed to fade so completely.

Joan Plowright played the leading role, Lady Pitts, as a cross between Lady Bracknell and the Madwoman of Chaillot, with overtones of Blanche Dubois. Slinging down the double brandies in a Soho restaurant, she invited all present home to tea. In Act II they arrived at her Hampstead fastness to discover that she had forgotten ever having met them. A good deal of philosophising ensued, especially when Olivier, as her aged millionaire husband, came wheeling in. Sadness prevailed. Suddenly the tone was recognisable: Anouilh, Fry, Rattigan. An unmistakable post-war *tristesse*, luxury of language offsetting the reality of rationing. The

97

rise of prosperity turned that whole strain of dramatic writing into a back number, but a lot of it was well written and actors were right to love playing it.

Kissinger on Communism (BBC2) featured the modern Metternich, introduced by David Brinkley and interviewed by our own Michael Charlton. Kissinger's strengths and weaknesses were equally to the fore. His analysis of the global strategic pattern was masterly. He was undoubtedly right in asserting that communism, all other things being equal, would always be outperformed by capitalism. But when it came to explaining why, in that case, communism should be making such advances in capitalist countries, he was stumped. He called it a paradox. It has obviously still not occurred to him that his own foreign policy was responsible for making the other side look good by comparison. Kissinger burns down Cambodia, delivers the people of Chile into the hands of torturers, and then wonders why young people in the democratic countries become disaffected.

22 January, 1978

Good hang

THE scene was Kitzbühel, the programme *Grandstand* (BBC1). The event was the Men's Downhill. A man referred to as 'Britain's sole representative' came plummeting down the Streif. 'He won't be looking for a first place today,' said David Vine, 'he'll be looking for experience.'

At that very instant – not a bit later, but *while David was actually saying it* – Britain's sole representative was upside down and travelling into the crowd at 60 m.p.h. plus. Spectators were mown down as if by grape-shot. The air was full of snow, beanies, mittens, bits of wood. You had to be watching to get the full impact. It was a kind of perfection. On television the great hours might take place on schedule, but the great moment can happen at any time.

The activities in *Ski Sunday* (BBC2) were likewise blessed with the redeeming presence of David Vine. The venue was Finland, the event was the 70-metre ski jump, and David had equipped himself with yet another new line in priapic dialogue. 'Got good hang,' David would intone, as a jumper standing horizontally to attention with a ski-tip in each nostril went sailing down the valley. The really important thing for a jumper was to have good hang. There was no point having the explosion if you did not have good hang.

'There's the explosion!' David would cry as the jumper launched himself into the void. 'Hang, hang, hang ... and that is *long*!' Kokkonen had extremely good hang and exploded enormously, but the man I liked was the one who lost a ski on the way down and had to choose between landing on the leg with the ski or the leg without. He chose the leg without – a huge error.

29 January–26 February, 1978

Tragic finish

ACCORDING to *Grandstand* (BBC1), Cambridge's sinking in the Boat Race was the biggest Easter tragedy in two thousand years.

Everything began normally with Oxford stroking along to their usual win, Cambridge on their way to oblivion and the crucifixion of Jesus Christ still likely to be the chief media talking-point over the weekend. But then tragedy struck. It struck gradually. First less and less of Cambridge's frail shell was showing above the choppy water, and then none at all, leaving the crew still rowing staunchly away but going nowhere except downwards. The commentator did his best to prepare us for our coming bereavement.

'It could be a sinking ... yes it is ... they've gone into the dolphin effect ... ' (There was no time to explain the dolphin effect. I suppose that when dolphins get into trouble they go into the Cambridge effect.) 'And now it's panic ... unbelievable how they could go down so quickly ... they're all still alive ... what a tragic finish ... '

Particularly impressive at this point was the way in which several of the Cambridge crew refused to give up, but went on rowing even though nothing still protruded from the water except their heads and shoulders. 'Unbelievable ... what drama we've had ... I'd like to see them get aboard and safe ... that water is *cold* ... '

Finally even the most determined crew-members latched on to the fact that their chance of completing the race was now slight. 'One or two grins ... maybe they're enjoying this ... let's go back to Oxford, because as far as they're concerned the race is still on ... and here are Oxford, triumphant Oxford, not *quite* a hollow victory ... '

It seemed to be all over. 'Scenes of jubilation at the finish ... 1951 was the last sinking, when Oxford sank ... this time it was Cambridge ... tragic ... ' But then the action replays started. 'Let's have another look at how this all ended ... in slow motion this time ... they were doomed from this moment ... '

2 April, 1978

Personal freedom

THE worst TV programme of this or any other week was the *Conservative Party Political Broadcast* (all channels), which twice referred to a Russian writer called Solzhenitskyn.

If Solzhenitskyn is against Socialism, we should be too: that was the message. The message was somewhat weakened by the fact that there is no such writer as Solzhenitskyn. The man they mean is called Solzhenitsyn – there is a 'ts' but there is no 'k'. The pronunciation 'Solzhenitskyn' was invented last year by Margaret Thatcher, who thereby suggested that she knew nothing about Solzhenitsyn's writings beyond what she had heard from her advisers, who in turn had apparently mixed him up with Rumpelstiltskin.

Other attractions of the Tory PPB included Reg Prentice, who was to be seen sitting in the path of a Force 10 gale, apparently in order to demonstrate that sparse, lank hair looks very ratty in a high wind. Possessing even less hair than Reg, I can advise him that the thing to do is cut it short. Growing it long and winding it round your head like a coil of rope is effective only if you fix the result with Araldite and wear a motor-cycle helmet when out of doors. Lectures on personal freedom lose force when delivered by someone who looks in desperate need of Supplementary Benefits.

The rest of the broadcast showed a comparable lack of judgment. It left you wondering, not for the first time, if the Tories any longer know quite what they're up to. *Are We Really Going to be Rich?* (Yorkshire) left you wondering if anybody else knows what he's up to either. A marathon drone-in with satellite link-ups, the show dealt with the challenge allegedly posed by the wealth purportedly about to emanate from North Sea oil.

Our host was David Frost, gripping his clip-board like a discobolus in mufti. He was on terrific form, cueing in savants from all over the world, cutting them off before they said enough to subtract from the confusion, switching to the studio audience whenever somebody sitting in it had something irrelevant he urgently wanted to contribute.

The component elements of his disarming physiognomy having been reassembled after a quick trip through space from California, Milton Friedman appeared in a big close-up on the studio wall. Friedman advised giving the money to the people, so that they could all become capitalists. Tony Benn appeared on the same wall, having been beamed line-of-sight from London. Benn advised using the money to revive British industry.

Sir Keith Joseph, present in the studio, argued for tax cuts so that the people would be encouraged to create more wealth in their turn. Benn's proposals, according to Sir Keith, would only mean throwing the money away on British Leyland. As a layman I am bound to say I thought this last point had force: there seems little point in sucking up money out of one hole only to squirt it down another.

These formidable men spoke with equal plausibility, which meant that you were progressively left just as puzzled as you were before, but presumably on an increasingly high level. All concerned were clear, literate, urbane. Only Lord Balogh sounded like an economist. From what you could understand of his message, it was old and tired. It was also probably right. If the State spends the money where it seems most needed, justice is at least aimed at, even if not necessarily achieved. The last Tory tax bonanza brought the country nothing but property speculation – the worst morale-killer of the lot.

'You are about to see something absolutely amazing,' said the voice-over introducing *Horizon* (BBC2). Amazing it was: a machine reading an ordinary printed book to a blind man. The secret was the silicon chip microprocessor, which is a way of connecting together about a quarter of a million transistors in a space the size of your fingernail. The result is a Lilliputian computer with endless implications for the future. Some of these have already started happening: the Swiss watch industry, for example, has been wiped out, and nobody now wants to buy any kind of mechanical calculator.

Almost everybody's job will be affected, up to and including doctors and lawyers. There was a disturbing sequence showing a famous American diagnostician teaching his life-time of experience to a silicon chip data bank. A big debate is already raging about whether Britain should try to build these things on its own account or simply confine itself to providing software – the programming and planning that we are already famous for. The issue was not settled on the programme and presumably won't be until taken up by David Frost. Will *his* job be affected? Will mine?

There is no reason why a television critic should not be replaced by a silicon chip if all he has to watch is stuff like *Miss England 1978* (BBC1), in which technology took over from people years ago. Android dancers programmed for maximum offensiveness mimed to the opening song. 'This is Miss England [Boo-ba-ba-*bum*], everything about her is LOVELY!'

Terry Wogan glided forward on silent wheels and introduced us to his mechanical companion, Ray Moore. A banter tape was unspooling somewhere in each stiffly smiling head. 'People will say we're in love, Terry.' 'He's a flatterer, but I like him. Go ahead, Ray.' Ray went ahead with the same eerie glide, disappearing behind the scenes in order to provide noises off.

Cyborgs in female attire wobbled towards camera while Ray (the name stands for Recycled Automatic Yammer) filled in on sound. 'Her great passion is watching golf. Pretty attractive *birdie* she is too.' The cyborgs still can't walk straight or turn corners but the technology for lip-licking and tongue-poking is obviously getting better all the time.

The Fiftieth Academy Awards (Thames) was a bad scene. It, too, had dancers. Bob Hope told weak jokes which everybody pretended to find funny. 'Nobody Does It Better' was gruesomely sung by Aretha Franklin, all talent and no taste. Vanessa Redgrave gave a terrible little speech, pledging her support in the fight against anti-Semitism and Fascism.

It was encouraging to be thus assured that anti-Semitism and Fascism are now doomed, but one couldn't help being depressed at Vanessa's evident failure to realise how snugly she fits into the showbiz world which she deludes herself that she stands out from. Like almost everyone else in the auditorium, she was an ego on the rampage. Woody Allen had the right idea: he stayed away.

9 April, 1978

Not by any means full

A MORE than usually cretinous annual instalment of *The Eurovision Song Contest* (BBC1) started the week with a phut. The venue, situated somewhere in Paris, was enough in itself to inspire dread.

In the 4,000-seat Palais des Congrès, strobe lights and lasers roamed and blinked while rather fewer than four thousand song-lovers assembled to appreciate this year's offerings. Terry Wogan, the Beeb's No. 1 front-man for such non-occasions, had an explanation for the empty places. 'Not by any means full – possibly for security reasons.' He didn't consider the possibility that the wiser ticket-holders had taken one look at the décor and gone home.

When Britain hosts the contest there is usually some attempt to provide a bilingual pitchperson: Katie Boyle, for example, or Angela Rippon. But the French indulge in no such fripperies. Their own lady – called, according to my notes, Denise Valve – stuck to the native language. Luckily for us, Terry was there to tell us what she was on about.

'A man is born to do one thing,' Colm C. T. Wilkinson of Ireland yelled desperately. 'And I was born to sing.' How wrong can a man be? 'That's a belter of a start,' Terry averred. Jahn Teigen of Norway, sporting chic pink punk-pants and a 100-year-old face, ended his song with a mid-air splits, just as Freddy used to do when he fronted the Dreamers. It was all like being dragged back through time to an era that was never very interesting in the first place.

An Italian group, conforming to the now standard Abba-style two-boy two-girl line-up, sang the classiest song of the night, 'Questo amore'. Unfortunately the sound balance was out of whack. It was even more so for the British entry. 'The Bad Old Days', sung by Co-Co. The drummer's vocal fills were twice as loud as anything coming from the lead singers. Were the Frog sound engineers trying to sabotage us? Not that 'The Bad Old Days' needed any sabotaging.

And so the evening ground on, with the dreadful familiarity of a recurring dream. In the great tradition of 'Boom-Bang-a-Bang', Denmark gave us a number entitled 'Boom-Boom'. Israel ran on to deliver a jaunty nonsense called 'A-Ba-Ni-Bi', which is doubtless the Hebrew for 'Boom-Bang-Boom-Bang' and has the additional virtue of echoing the word 'Abba'. Anyway, Israel won, but long before the votes were counted I switched over to *The South Bank Show* (LWT), where Melvyn Bragg was extracting, drop by drop, a fascinating interview from Harold Pinter.

It was exactly like getting blood out of a stone, except that stones do not smoke. Pinter smoked all the time. You could tell that the interview was edited down from hours of film because in every shot Pinter had a fresh Balkan Sobranie in his hand. In the tight head-shots there was so much smoke pouring up from the bottom of the screen that you began wondering if his trousers were on fire.

Winning a charm contest against Melvyn Bragg is not easy, but Pinter never looked like losing. He made it disarmingly plain that he had no pretensions towards understanding what his own work means. Something in life creates a lasting image in his mind. In the course of time the image wants to become a play. The play gets written, after which it no longer has much to do with him. Beyond that he wasn't able to discuss the matter. Questions about his themes and working methods consequently led nowhere. 'I'm getting nowhere,' declared Melvyn. 'No,' said the voice in the smoke.

Questions about his life, however, drew answers that told

you a lot about Pinter's peculiar verbal force. Describing how Fascists used to chase him during his East End childhood, he recalled some lines of dialogue with which he once extricated himself from a close encounter. It sounded exactly like a scene from *The Birthday Party*. His ear for what really gets said when things like that happen is what makes him an interesting writer.

The advantage of working entirely from instinct is that the incongruities of actuality are not smoothed down by reason. The disadvantage is that the instinct can't tell a strong theme from a weak one. In a play like *The Birthday Party* Pinter is dealing with a central experience – being hunted down and crushed by a superior power – that nobody in the twentieth century is likely to find trivial. But his love-game plays for television I find as wearisome as being told someone else's nightmare.

First-rate artists usually think as well as feel: they are invariably their own best critics. Pinter, a slave to his inspiration, can do nothing except 'let it run ... let it happen'. It's a kind of irresponsibility which often arouses, in at least one viewer of his work, a perfect fury of disapproval. But at least, as this halting yet strangely fruitful conversation showed, the irresponsibility is obtained within a responsible man.

30 April, 1978

Chewing the sporran

CONSIDERING that ancient Athens was crammed with philosophers who had nothing to do with their time except sit around thinking up words, it's no wonder that the Greeks had a word for it. The word is hubris.

Once England's hopes of competing in the World Cup had vanished, it was an understandable case of transferred nationalism that the English, instantly restyling themselves the British, should heap Scotland with the burden of national expectations. But it was hubris to be so confident that Scotland would do well. Television, during the past week, has not been as bad as the Press in pouring scorn on Ally and his army, but it was at least as bad in the way it built them up in the first place. The best you can say in mitigation is that the Scots themselves showed less judgment than anybody.

Anyway, you had your choice of channels on which to view the unfolding disaster. For the connoisseur of high drama, the BBC was, as usual, the better bet. The Saturday afternoon preludes to the Scotland–Peru match were referred to by Dickie Davies of ITV as 'the build-up to and coverage of the big one'. Unfortunately Dickie, after announcing the build-up to and coverage of the big one, disappeared from the screen, resurfacing only to provide links. On the Beeb Frank Bough was there all the time. 'What a day it must be to be a Scotsman,' he mused ecstatically. There was no getting rid of him. When Jimmy Hill and the experts showed up, Frank was right there with them.

Videotape of past triumphs was resurrected, principally in order to demonstrate a quality known as Scotland's Power in the Air. There were awed voices-over from the assembled experts. 'Dalglish ... I don't think any player but Dalglish could have got in there ... I don't think anybody in the world ... Dalglish.' The experts, referred to by Frank as 'some great characters', were unanimous.

Out in Argentina, David Coleman chimed in, telling us, with no apparent sense of impending doom, that Ally MacLeod had described his own goalkeeper as 'one of the best in the World Cup' and his own midfield as 'one of the best in the world'. The tune began changing when the Peruvians, one goal down, suddenly revealed an ability to run faster with the ball than the Scots could run without it. When Peru levelled, the Scots back home must have been regurgitating their haggis.

'We are really watching a fascinating game of football,' said Frank at half-time. For once he was right. On ITV Kevin Keegan said: 'I think they've got problems.' Referring to the Peruvians, Paddy Crerand said: 'They've frightened the life out of me.' The charming Andy Gray looked equally distraught. A disarming trio, these, but I craved the madder music of the Beeb, switching back just in time to hear David say: 'Dalglish, who's so far made little impression.'

After several mentions of the hole in Asa Hartford's heart, David referred to him as a 'whole-hearted player', but managed to get in an apology before the BBC switchboard broke down completely. David, at least, was on form. So, alas, was Peru. They saved a penalty – another sporran-chewing moment for the watching Scots. The second Peruvian goal must have had them hitting each other with cabers. 'Sad the way this match has drifted away from Scotland,' murmured David. I suppose there was a Roman commentator saying the same kind of thing at Cannae. 'Sad the way this battle has drifted away from the legions.'

'You've got to admit the best team won,' said Keegan on ITV. 'They could have by a lot more.' It was agreed that it was 'unfortunate that there are so many short players in the Scottish team'. The mysterious evaporation of Scotland's Power in the Air was thus explained. Back on the Beeb, Ally MacLeod bravely spoke to David, regretting his team's 'pure performance'. There was no point in asking him to be mure specific. That it was indeed a pure performance was not to be ignured.

Two days of recriminations followed, exacerbated by Willie Johnston's little blunder with the pills. Willie flew home to be dressed down by Frank Bough. 'You shouldn't be here at all, should you? You should be out there playing World Cup football for Scotland. How do you feel?' But by now it was time for the build-up to the coverage of an even bigger one, Scotland v. Iran. Once again hubris was thick on the ground. Scotland would need to win by a lot of goals if they were going to qualify. Some darker voices suggested that they might win by only a few goals. Only the known Cassandras – mad creatures with rent garments and tresses in disarray – dared to speculate that Scotland might not win at all.

Scattered thinly in the stands, Scots fans with drooping dirks and detumescent Tam o' Shanters spent a lot of time watching Joe Jordan falling over. On ITV, voice-overs detected 'a certain lack of spirit in the Scottish side'. The Iranians, an amateur squad consisting largely of policemen, catering officers, hairdressers and interior decorators, should have been able to lose comfortably, but in the event could not quite manage it, even after putting a shot through their own goal.

In the chill aftermath, Andy Gray said that Scotland's attitude was wrong. 'We in the media,' said Brian Moore, 'didn't help there.' He could say that again. Unfortunately he didn't, but I hope there will be others to say it again for him. Just because some of the Scots fans are silly enough to mortgage their houses is no reason for experienced mediamen to go so far out on the same limb. In fact it was one of the Glasgow fans, interviewed in the street, who finally put the truth in a nutshell. 'They should have had the send-off after they came back.'

11 June, 1978

Something of themselves

'So tomorrow is the longest day,' murmured Alastair Burnet at the end of Tuesday night's *News at Ten* (ITN), 'which means that the nights will soon be drawing in.' Reginald Bosanquet gazed at him in wonder.

The urge of telly regulars to give us something of themselves is understandable. The longer the time they have to spend waiting around, and the less opportunity they have to say anything significant once they get on, the keener they are to assert their personalities. The most desperate cases are the regional link-men, who spend all day in the studio for a total air-time of less than a minute. Hence their horrible jauntiness. 'Well, I don't know about you, but I ... ' 'And I know I'm not the only one who can't get enough of those floppy, furry ... ' 'That's all from me.'

What is it about Dickie Davies (*World of Sport*, LWT) that makes you feel less wretched about Frank Bough (*Grandstand*, BBC1)? By any rational standards, Frank ought to be definitively awful: the whole time that his stupefying ebullience is sending you to sleep, his RANDOM use of emphasis is JERK-ing you awake. Dickie doesn't do any of that. On the contrary, he speaks with exactly the same degree of measured excitement about every sporting event that turns up on a Saturday afternoon anywhere in the world. Perhaps that's the trouble.

Understandably keen about the World Cup, Dickie folds his hands, leans forward and smiles at you from under his moustache. Equally keen about the World Target Clown Diving Championships, he folds his hands, leans forward, and smiles at you from under his moustache. Transmitted from Florida, the World Target Clown Diving Championship features half a dozen local stunt-men in fancy dress somersaulting 200 feet into a wet handkerchief.

Any mad American pseudo-sport is grist to *World of Sport*'s mill. Souped-up tractors have tugs-of-war against hang-gliders. In the World Bus Jumping Classic – brought to you direct from Tampax, Arizona – a man tries to jump a bus over a hundred motorcycles. The attempt is unsuccessful. Flames leap up from the shattered bus. Men in asbestos suits rush forward, their poised nozzles disgorging foam. Back to Dickie, who folds his hands, leans forward, and smiles at you from under his moustache.

It was instructive to compare the levels of hysteria when

the BBC and ITV were both supplying live coverage of the same World Cup match. The BBC had the decibels and ITV had the information. In fact ITV, despite frequent appearances by Brian Clough, outperformed the BBC in every department throughout the World Cup. None of this stopped me watching the Beeb, however. It isn't just that there are no commercials and no Dickie. It's something deeper, something occult, something to do with the personality of David Coleman. Just by being so madly keen, he helps you get things in proportion. Anything that matters so much to David Coleman, you realise, doesn't really matter much at all.

The two great mysteries of the World Cup were the gloves worn by Sepp Maier, West Germany's goalkeeper. They were enormous. He didn't have to crouch very far before the tips of his gloves brushed the ground. When he held them up, they filled the goal. Are the hands inside them the same size? Alas, West Germany was eliminated before this question could be resolved.

The Argentina v. Peru match was marvellous. To prove this, David Coleman described the transports, variously expressed according to national temperament, of his fellow craftsmen in the commentary box. 'The commentators going *mad*!' Suddenly you had a dazzling vision of all the world's David Colemans going mad in their different ways: shouting, gesticulating, dumping ashes on their heads, disembowelling themselves, etc. Köhlmann, Ko-Lu-Man, Caldamano, Kulamundis ...

At half-time, with Argentina two up, Frank Bough invited us to share the excitement 'as the World Cup reaches an absolute PINnacle'. Then it was back to the stadium to watch the footballers provide suitable illustrations for David's commentary. This wasn't always easy, but they usually managed it. 'The story gets better and better!' screamed David, and it actually did. After Argentina got the fourth goal, David yelled: 'Argentina will meet Holland in the final!' Then it must have occurred to him that Argentina's four-goal lead, the necessary margin if they were to qualify, would be lessened if Peru managed to snatch a goal back. 'It can't be forgotten that Argentina can't afford to concede goals!' He was the only man in the world who had forgotten it, but no matter.

And so the home team swept on to victory. Already General Videla was looking like the Father of His Country. If Argentina wins this afternoon, he will be a world statesman. Let's hope that the benefits of the host nation's dizzy success will spread all the way to the jails. Perhaps some of the innocent people locked up in them will be tortured a bit more gently from now on. Meanwhile it is hard not to be reminded of German sporting performances before World War II, when the all-conquering Mercedes-Benz and Auto Union racing cars persuaded the world that Hitler couldn't be all bad. Oh yes he could.

On the *South Bank Show* (LWT), Melvyn Bragg introduced a long and excellent programme about Kenneth MacMillan's ballet *Mayerling*, profusely illustrated with excerpts from the work itself. It has been argued that we should have been given the whole ballet, but if that had happened there would have been no time to watch Lynn Seymour and David Wall rehearsing. Try as I might, I can't be Dickie Davies about Lynn Seymour. I am Frank Bough about her. Sometimes I go completely David Coleman just looking at her. Just standing there, she is not particularly shapely or even pretty, but when she moves she somehow becomes simultaneously ethereal and sexy, like a Platonic concept in Janet Reger underwear.

25 June, 1978

Unbearable suffrage

HALF a century of women's suffrage was celebrated by *Golden Gala* (ATV), a blockbusting, ball-breaking variety show that left at least one male viewer clutching his groin with fright. They're out to get us, chaps.

With the participation of more than a hundred female stars, what *TV Times* called 'the all-woman super-show' was staged at the London Palladium in the presence of Princess Margaret, a dedicated lady well accustomed to displaying a gracious smile of appreciation when people in the world of the arts line up to bore her. But by this event even she must have had her patience taxed beyond endurance. Even if they do nothing but call out their name, rank and serial number, it takes a certain amount of time for more than a hundred female stars to file past a given point. If each of them is deputed to sing a song, read a speech or take part in a sketch, it follows inevitably that the procession will last all night.

In a uniformly dire compilation of acts, the sketches stood out by being even more dreadful than the songs. Actresses from *The Rag Trade*, with Miriam Karlin to the fore, did a turn wherein the position of women in politics was supposedly illuminated. 'You can always trust a politician who smokes a pipe,' somebody said – or it could have been, 'You can never trust a politician who smokes a pipe,' it doesn't matter. The remark was greeted with a hurricane of laughter.

'Mrs Thatcher doesn't smoke a pipe,' somebody else said. This remark was greeted with an uproar of enthusiasm and prolonged applause, as if Pericles had just concluded an address to the Athenians by performing the Hammerklavier Sonata. 'She would if she thought it would get her a few more votes,' said whoever had been entrusted with the punchline. This remark was overwhelmed by a mass paroxysm of hysterical delight which if it had been elicited by Hitler would have scared him off the podium.

The deeper significance of such material consisted in the satisfaction being taken from the fact that women were now free to be as cynical as men. The same line of thought kept surfacing throughout the show. Female liberty kept being defined in male terms. The paradox, if it is one, was especially apparent in the musical items, starting off with a production number of 'There is Nothing Like a Dame'. The song had been updated with some limply apposite lyrics, but it defiantly remained a male chauvinist pig's snorting hymn to the intuitive, cute and tender unpredictability of the sow.

As a logical extension of the same idea, women dressed themselves up to look as sexy as possible and then presumed to despise men for lusting after them. A squad of angry black girls ran on stage in order to gyrate arousingly while pouring scorn on any male who might be foolish enough to classify them as sex objects. 'You'd better stop your fantasisin' ' they instructed us shrilly. For those of us who hadn't been doin' any fantasisin', the advice was supererogatory at best.

Up at the other end of the market, where long gowns are worn, distinguished ladies introduced each other's numbers with fulsome accolades. If the lady had no number of her own to perform, she made a performance out of introducing somebody else's number. 'We all serve in different ways,' said Noele Gordon. 'Ladies and gentlemen, here is someone very special.' As Ms Gordon serenely tackled the job of getting herself and her gown off stage, the curtains opened to reveal Mary O'Hara, who once again favoured the world with that song in which two cuckoos discuss their respective life-styles ('Will there be danger to us from the hawk?') before embarking on a course of self-fulfilment. I like Mary, but she overdoes the dirndls.

Petula Clark, billed above everybody else, climaxed the evening with majestic inappropriateness by singing 'I Don't Know How to Love Him' from *Jesus Christ, Superstar*. As

always with Petula, the technique was as perfect as the emotions were suspect. She pretended to have a little cry at the
end. Some of us out in the audience were crying for real. Like
many men of my generation I am grateful to the feminist
movement for helping to release us from the burden of male
supremacy: whatever the purported revolution in women's
consciousness might have led to, the change in men's minds
has surely been a blessing.

It is good to see women being independent, since it means
that men are freed from some of the more tiresome obligations
of being dominant. But it is not good to see our newly liberated sisters making idiots of themselves. *Golden Gala* was the
bummer of the century. It put the feminist movement back
fifty years at least. After this, they'll have to start chaining
themselves to railings again and committing suicide at Epsom.

16 July, 1978

Carry on creating

'A STOLEN moment of passion produced a child named
Mavis.' Each episode of *Best Seller: A Testimony of Two
Men* (Thames) starts with a synopsis full of lines like that.
The series is hopeless, but the synopsis is terrific.

In *Clouds of Glory* (Granada) Ken Russell, assisted by
Melvyn Bragg, gave us a two-part study of Wordsworth and
Coleridge respectively. Wordsworth was the tall, spotty one,
played by David Warner. Coleridge was shorter and fell
about. He was incarnated by David Hemmings.

The first episode was somewhat subdued for Ken Russell.
When Wordsworth appeared, he was not attired in Nazi
uniform. But the way he lurched towards camera instantly
identified the film as being by Russell. After lurching towards
camera, Wordsworth lurched away from it across the fells,

shouting at them in blank verse. Dorothy Wordsworth, played by Felicity Kendall, flashed her fanny through a muslin negligee.

Cut to the French Revolution. Lying on top of Annette Vallon, Wordsworth addresses her in lyrical cadences while the camera gets a close-up of his skin problem. Suddenly the French Revolution comes bursting through the door. Disillusion.

Back at the Lakes, Wordsworth slowly recovers the urge to Create. 'You moost eat, Willyum,' says Dorothy, 'and you moost start writing again.' For Ken and Melvyn, the unimaginable thing is to stop Creating. The manifest truth that Wordsworth Created far too much obviously crossed neither of their minds. Points should be awarded, however, for their restraint in not sending William and Dorothy to bed together. The biographical details were left largely unaltered, distortion being confined to the fundamentals. Chief of these was the assumption that Wordsworth's poetry had everything to do with the spontaneous overflow of powerful feelings but nothing at all to do with emotion recollected in tranquillity.

With Coleridge Ken let it all hang out. Getting himself mixed up with the Ancient Mariner and Sarah mixed up with the albatross, Coleridge stabbed her through the heart with what looked like the nineteenth century's only example of an aluminium anchor, which he had got mixed up with a cross-bow. That was just the start. The rest was a long tussle between Coleridge and the demon opium. The latter got the upper hand, but Coleridge fought back. He screamed. He fell down. He got up. He sent his books crashing to the floor. He sold his books for more opium. He did everything with his books except read them.

Nor did he spend much time writing. Apart from outright hysteria, the highest common factor uniting Ken Russell's films about great artists is the way you never get any idea of the greatest artist sitting down to work. One of the things that make great artists great is their capacity to escape the confines of their personal lives and speak for us all. But in Ken's view a great artist's art is always just his personality intensified. Brave, committed and adventurous though he be, Ken is essentially a scandalmonger.

I liked *Will Shakespeare* (ATV) and am sorry to see it end. It had its crudities, but was blessedly devoid of scandal. Most of the events dreamed up by John Mortimer could easily be imagined as having happened. Events just like them, indeed, happen to everyone. Shakespeare's uniqueness lay in the power with which he expressed the realisation that he was not unique. Merrily bashing out his lines of pewter, Mortimer was yet careful to give Shakespeare a believably ordinary life. Tim Curry brilliantly took the opportunity to portray a man of small outward show and vast inner resources. The scene in which Shakespeare and Queen Elizabeth recognised each other's stature was entirely convincing.

In the series of lectures on *Multi-Racial Britain* (BBC2), the outstanding paper was delivered by Dr Bikhu Parekh. Previous speakers had aired most of the issues but he was the one who gave them shape. The triumph of his speech was its positive character. He did not content himself with merely denouncing the idea of repatriation as a trade in human beings. He argued, surely with good reason, that immigration had already been a boon and could well bring about a revival of this country's waning energies.

Dr Parekh contended, again surely with good reason, that the English character no longer enjoys diversity. In the nicest possible way, but firmly and inexorably, he shifted the focus of attention to where it belongs. The clarity of his forensic manner was a lesson in itself. For people apt to delude themselves that Enoch Powell is a distinguished speaker, here was an example of what a truly distinguished speaker sounds like.

A Falstaff in the same enlightened army of which men like Dr Parekh are the commanders, George Gale went on *Thames at Six* (Thames) to denounce youngsters who wear

Nazi arm-bands when they go to the pub. 'I always leave immediately,' growled George. It went without saying that for George to leave a pub is no casual gesture. *Thames at Six* is probably a more interesting grab-bag than *Nationwide* (BBC1), although if you button-punch between them it is sometimes hard to remember which item happened on what.

For bad taste, *Thames at Six* unquestionably has the edge. A few days ago it produced Judy Carne, fresh from her car-crash and still suffering from a broken neck. A steel halo brace, weighing 20 lb., enclosed her head like a silver cage. It was bolted directly into her forehead. Somewhere inside all this she was still being tirelessly vivacious. 'They give me medicine for it. I'm really not in pain at all.' Since *Laugh-In*, Judy Carne's career has gone as haywire as Kathy Kirby's. For famous people who fail to protect themselves there seems to be no mercy.

Nationwide featured an amazing collection of apprentice impersonators. From all over Britain, schoolchildren materialised via local studios to give us their imitations of the mighty. There were at least three uncannily accurate Margaret Thatchers, their eyelids fatigued with condescension and their voices swooping and whining like dive-bombers. A boy still in short pants did an Eddie Waring that soared into airy realms of abstract enunciation. He was better at it than Mike Yarwood, having noticed how Eddie's voice abruptly gets louder or softer as he sways behind the microphone.

A girl did a dazzling Shirley Bassey, her mouth suddenly appearing under one ear. For the ten minutes that the kids were on, *Nationwide* was a better variety programme than anything the Beeb has recently been able to come up with later in the evening. There was even some sincere laughter from Frank Bough. You can tell when he is laughing sincerely. He looks normal.

In *Rhythm on Two* (BBC2) Marion Montgomery quietly demonstrated that she possesses Blossom Dearie's touch, Cleo Laine's technique, and an elegantly judged oomph all of her own. On *Elkie & Co* (Thames), Elkie Brooks demonstrated that a rock queen with half the equipment of Marion Montgomery can become ten times as big a star. Elkie used to be a raunchy singer with Vinegar Joe, a band that looked like an angry armpit. Now she has a wardrobe of frocks by Ossie Clark and Zandra Rhodes. She has been cleaned up, rubbed down, reined in and tricked out. Let's hope it all pays off.

23 July, 1978

Green beef

UNLIKE Bionic Woman or Six Million Dollar Man *The Incredible Hulk* (ITV) is not a rebuild but a true mutant. Bionic and Six used to be ordinary human beings but were transformed by engineering. Hulk remains an ordinary human being who can't help turning into an extraordinary one every time he gets angry. An 'overdose of gamma radiation' has altered 'his body chemistry' so that in vexing moments he becomes the physical expression of his own fury.

'The creature', it is explained, 'is driven by rage.' A combination of Clark Kent and Dr Jekyll, 'mild-mannered' David Banner falls first into a sweat, then into a trance, and finally into a metamorphosis. In the same time that it takes to wheel a small actor off and a large one on, a weedy schnurk like you and me is transmogrified into seven feet of green beef.

Hulk has the standard body-builder's physique, with two sets of shoulders one on top of the other and wings of lateral muscle that hold his arms out from his sides as if his armpits had piles. He is made remarkable by his avocado complexion, eyes like plover's eggs and the same permanently exposed lower teeth displayed by Richard Harris when he is acting determined, or indeed just acting.

Given a flying start by the shock effect of his personal apperance. Hulk goes into action against the heavies, flinging them about in slow motion. Like Bionic, Six and Wonderwoman, Hulk does his action numbers at glacial speed. Emitting slow roars of rage, Hulk runs very slowly towards the enemy, who slowly attempt to make their escape. But no matter how slowly they run, Hulk runs more slowly. Slowly he picks them up, gradually bangs their heads together, and with a supreme burst of lethargy throws them through the side of a building.

Hardly have the bricks floated to the ground before Hulk is changing back into spindly David, with a sad cello weeping on the sound-track. One thinks of Frankenstein's monster or the Hunchback of Nôtre Dame. One thinks of King Kong. One thinks one is being had. Why can't the soft twit cut the soul-searching and just enjoy his ability to swell up and clobber the foe? But David is in quest of 'a way to control the raging spirit that dwells within him'. Since the series could hardly continue if he finds it, presumably he will be a long time on the trail.

If you took the violence out of American television there wouldn't be much left, and if you took the American television out of British television there wouldn't be much left of that either. Without imported series, our programme planners couldn't fill the schedules. Whether schedules ought to be filled is another question. As things stand, American series have to be bought in. Nearly all of them are violent to some degree. But those who believe that violence on television causes violence in real life should take consolation from the fact that most of the violence in American series is on a par with the Incredible Hulk torpidly jumping up and down on the langorously writhing opponents of freedom and justice.

It's British programmes that show life's dark underside. In American programmes, however full of crashed cars and flying bodies, the values remain unswervingly wholesome.

You can't imagine the Americans making a series like *Out* (Thames). I found myself wishing that the British hadn't made it either. Having missed the early episodes, I was a bit behind the story when I finally tuned in, so perhaps the thread escaped me. Certainly the atmospherics deserved all the praise they got: Tom Bell and the other actors reeked of bad diet and even the air looked dirty. But the events seemed unlikely. The hit-man who blew up the hero's car was the only person on the scene after the explosion. Common sense told you that everyone in the district would have been on the scene and the hit-man would have been somewhere else.

Authenticity was reserved for the torture scenes. A grass had his kidney's knuckled by the hero's friend. This was all too believable. Lest we miss any of it, the camera moved in tight on the victim's face. One of my reasons for not joining panels or accepting invitations to give lectures is that I simply don't know whether television ought to show things as they are or as they ought to be. Moreover I don't trust anybody who thinks he does know.

On the whole it is probably wiser to show that hitting somebody really hurts him, instead of just making him drift lazily through the air. But there were times during the latest *Z-Cars* (BBC1) when watching, say, *Cannon* seemed very preferable. As some foul-spoken dockside stripper cowered at the prospect of having a steel comb shoved up her nose, it was impossible not to yearn for the magic land in which Cannon – the original and still the most incredible of all hulks – struggles from his car, plods after the fleeing thugs, and fells them with karate chops from his marshmallow hands.

Jane Fonda (BBC1) inhabits the same country. She is, in fact, a radicalised version of Wonderwoman. Having brought the war in Vietnam to an end, she is justifiably still awe-stricken at the change in her personality which made it all possible. It goes without saying – or rather it goes with a lot of saying – that the details of how she changed from a sex object into a political demiurge are of prime concern to the world.

I believe most of what Jane Fonda believes. In fact I believed most of it before she did. But after you have heard a few of your own liberal opinions coming out of Jane's mouth you start wondering whether the John Birch Society is so bad after all. Like Vanessa Redgrave, Jane seems to think that the state of her own ego is of fundamental importance to the history of the human race. Truly their collaboration in the film *Julia* was a conjunction of the mind and opposition of the stars.

'People were asking: "Where is Barbarella?"' piped Jane. Actually nobody was asking that. Nobody gave a stuff about Barbarella. But conceit must be forgiven in any woman married to a man like Tom Hayden. 'She has an intensity like no one you'll ever see,' he informed us, referring sternly to 'the agony of a life-change', while neglecting to examine the question of whether her earlier incarnation – the one that married Vadim and made idiotic movies like *Barbarella* – did so from choice.

The tacit assumption seemed to be that everyone was like that then: the whole culture was to blame. 'I think that she's changed in the sense that she's *evolved*.' Jane was ready to go along with that. 'I ... I ... me ... I felt *unworthy* ... very much a part of my whole being.' There is a lot to admire in Jane Fonda, but people so keen to tell you how they've changed never really change.

3 September, 1978

Holocaust

IT can't be done and perhaps ought never to have been attempted, but if you leave those questions aside then there should be room to admit the possibility that *Holocaust* (BBC1) wasn't really all that bad. At its best it gave a modicum of dramatic life to some notoriously intractable moral issues, and even at its worst was no disgrace.

One's chief objection to the film *Judgement at Nuremberg* and the TV blockbuster *QB VII* was not that they were cynical, but that their sincerity was mentally deficient. Approaching their frightful topic with a plenitude of reverence but an insufficiency of penetration, they left it less comprehensible than it had been before. *Judgement at Nuremberg* somehow encouraged the belief that the Nazis were a lot of cruel men who ganged up on Judy Garland, while *QB VII* gave the impression that the whole nightmare of the Third Reich had taken place in order to help a Hollywood screeen-writer solve his drinking problem.

The opening sequence of *Holocaust* suggested that it might be headed down the same road. The scene was a wedding party. One's first thought was of *The Godfather*. One's second thought, following hard on the heels of the first, was that we were in for a long barrage of schlock, since the sure sign of a schlock media product is that it is drawn not from life but from previous media products.

But things picked up. Let it be admitted that no character existed nor action took place except to make a point. What mattered was that most of the points were good. We were shown the Weiss family being slow to understand the fate that was overtaking them. It could be said that 1935 was a bit late for the Weisses to be embarking with such optimism on a mixed marriage. More trepidation would have been in order. But the general issue was not fudged.

The Weisses, and by implication all the Jews in Germany, were shown as being victims of wishful thinking. They thought that everything would come right. No reasonable person could doubt that what was happening could not continue. As with Stalin's Great Terror, only a madman could guess what was on the way. Even the perpetrators had to go one step at a time, completing each step before they realised that the next one was possible.

The German Jews were the most assimilated in Europe. They were vital to Germany's culture – which, indeed, has never recovered from their extinction. They couldn't see that they were hated in direct proportion to their learning, vitality and success. In the first episode the Weiss family, representing the Jews, played Viennese classical music on a Bechstein. In the last episode the Dorf family, representing the Nazis, picked out Christmas carols on the same Bechstein. The point was not laboured and indeed would have survived being made more firmly. Though they claimed to be purifying it, the Nazis were in fact engaged in the destruction of Germany's artistic heritage. They were dunces.

The aridity of the Nazi mind was the biggest poser the authors had to face. In creating Erik Dorf they went some way towards overcoming it. Played with spellbinding creepiness by Michael Moriarty, Erik spoke his murderous euphemisms in a voice as juiceless as Hitler's prose or Speer's architecture. Hitler's dream of the racially pure future was of an abstract landscape tended by chain-gangs of shadows and criss-crossed with highways bearing truckloads of Aryans endlessly speeding to somewhere undefined. Dorf sounded just like that: his dead mackerel eyes were dully alight with a limitless vision of banality.

Dorf began as an opportunist and ended as a fanatic. There was a contradiction in there somewhere, perhaps arising from the authors' otherwise commendable desire to cover all the themes. It is difficult to evoke outlandish crimes while simultaneously arguing that the criminals need not necessarily have been freaks. In her great book *Eichmann in Jerusalem* Hannah Arendt proposed that the truly frightening thing about Eichmann was his mediocrity. The makers of *Holocaust* had obviously grasped this point, but Dorf's low blink-rate and computerised voice were as close as they could go to giving it dramatic presence.

Eichmann himself was portrayed as a hard man who might have emanated from some German crime series called *Aus*.

Curling his waxen top lip – which counts as a neat trick – Tom Bell made reference to a Nazi hierarch called Gorbals, who unfortunately did not appear. In real life, if that's the phrase, Eichmann fancied himself as an expert on Jewish culture and saw his 'task' as being mainly one of keeping the trains running on time. What was in them was a side issue. There can be no doubt that he would have served just as devotedly if they had been loaded with bags of beans. The script should have made the point. Better writers would have found a way.

On the other hand it was impossible to imagine how an exotic character like Himmler could have been made both authentic and plausible. Forgivably, they settled for making him plausible, giving the role to Ian Holm and throttling back the full power of the Reichsführer's mania. Himmler was certainly banal, but he was also baroque, steaming around in a special train and diverting large amounts of the Third Reich's increasingly thin resources to such 'tasks' as proving scholastically that the Japanese were Aryans. How could you show all that and be believed? The whole Nazi reality was a caricature. The more precisely you evoke it, the less probable it looks.

Other kinds of incredibility were more avoidable. Rudi and Helena were believable as spectators at Babi Yar, but not as instant lovers. Certainly the senior Jews in Warsaw went on co-operating for an unconscionable time, but did Josef Weiss have to be quite such a dummy? Even here, though, it is important to say that matters were being fumbled, not fudged. The script bravely faced the lamentable fact that Jewish police killed their own people in Warsaw. Nor did it succumb to the now fashionable illusion that survivalism is somehow to be applauded. There were failures in expressive means, but not in moral imagination.

The use of language was never better than adequate. As in all hack writing, the dialogue showed no sense of period. Prodigies of set-dressing were undone by a phrase. Erik Dorf, talking about 'a few ideas I've been kicking around', sounded like a post-war Madison Avenue advertising executive. Going part way to make up the deficiency of good lines was the brilliance of some of the acting. Meryl Streep, as Inga Helms Weiss, was given the burden of being the Good German. She gave an astounding performance.

There is no hope that the boundless horror of Nazi Germany can be transmitted entire to the generations that will succeed us. There is a limit to what we can absorb of other people's experience. There is also a limit to how guilty we should feel about being unable to remember. Santayana was probably wrong when he said that those who forget the past are condemned to relive it. Those who remember are condemned to relive it too. Besides, freedoms are not guaranteed by historians and philosophers, but by a broad consent among the common people about what constitutes decent behaviour. Decency means nothing if it is not vulgarised. Nor can the truth be passed on without being simplified. The most we can hope for is that it shall not be travestied. *Holocaust* avoided that.

10 September, 1978

Manganese nodules

P REOCCUPIED last week with weightier matters, I had no space to examine a strange new type of programme currently invading the schedules. I mean the Very Boring Programme.

The Very Boring Programme seems to take pride in being as narcotic as possible. Special writers are hired to ensure that any potentially interesting idea is ironed flat and that anything flat is made paralysing. A case in point was a *Horizon* (BBC2) dealing with manganese nodules.

Manganese nodules, it appears, litter the ocean floor. 'Very little about them', said the voice-over, 'is yet certain.' There was consequently ample scope for referring to 'the enigma of manganese nodules'. Footage of nodules being tested was accompanied by an assurance that this was only one phase in what should rightfully be considered as 'a many-pronged scientific attack on the nodule enigma'.

Whence came the manganese nodule? Some say that the manganese nodule is a faecal pellet. Some say not. A sea-bed laboratory, or nodule module, was shown working on the vexed question of the manganese nodule's provenance. 'They vary in every possible respect.' Nodules were produced in order to back up this contention. One nodule was described as being 'what is known in nodule jargon as hamburger-shaped'. The possibility that some hamburgers might be what is known in hamburger jargon as nodule-shaped was not considered.

A theory that manganese nodules might be of riverine origin was advanced only to be discounted. 'Neither does the river theory hold water.' But you begin to see what I mean. After more than an hour of hearing about 'these humble blackish stones', confidently described as belonging to 'the common heritage of mankind', you had barely enough energy left to ask what the ulterior motive was. What were the programme-makers after? Perhaps they were trying to find out how much we could take without running amok.

After a week or so of reasonably normal scheduling, another Very Boring Programme showed up, once again on BBC2. It was called *Skateboard Kings*. There ought to be at least a few interesting things to say about what a skateboard is and how to ride it. One was even prepared to hear details of a many-pronged scientific attack on the skateboard enigma. Instead the programme elected to celebrate the skateboarding 'life-style'.

As opposed to life, which is various, a life-style concentrates on one activity and flogs it to death. Californian youths with head-bands were shown sleeping in their clothes and waking up for a new day. You could tell they were waking up because they rubbed their eyes with their fists, stretched, yawned, etc. Their plan was to bale out a swimming pool so that they could do 'incredible things' in it with their skateboards. There would have been some point in showing us these incredible things. Alas, what we saw mostly consisted of the swimming pool being baled out. Trash-cans were employed as baling devices. 'I'm gonna get a better trash-can,' cried one youth. 'There's a better trash-can up there.' Then he ran up there and got the trash-can.

Thus, by ingenuity and determination, the skateboard kings overcame the obstacles set for them by society. 'All those jerks really loused it up for us,' they averred. 'They're so hyperactive, man.' The skateboard kings didn't make the mistake of letting too much skateboarding get in the road of more important activities such as acting out their life-style with the assistance of improvised dialogue. 'Skateboarding is a gas,' they told each other. 'It's what I dig to do.' Surfing movies like *Tubular Swells* similarly tend towards philosophical speculation, but are usually careful to include some surfing. *Skateboard Kings* was like a surfing movie with the water let out.

A pot-holing series called *Beneath the Pennines* (BBC2) has manifested all the characteristics of a Very Boring Programme, but occasionally errs in the direction of being moderately engaging. The latest episode, dealing with Alum Pot, was billed as having won first prize at the Grenoble International Pot-holing Film Festival. This piece of news was in itself sufficient to stimulate the imagination. One was keen to see something of what goes on at the Grenoble International Pot-holing Film Festival. You could imagine the spectators lowering themselves into an auditorium situated somewhere deep beneath Grenoble, with stalactites in the foyer.

Alum Pot was less of a thrill, although not to be viewed

with entire equanimity. More than, or it could have been almost, 200 feet deep, it was formed 'some 15,000 years ago' and is so large that 'you could lose a 20-storey block of flats inside it.' Certainly you can lose any number of pot-holers inside it. They die down there all the time. There are three separate routes to destruction. On the shallowest there are excellent chances of bouncing from one slimy shelf to another and on the steepest you get an opportunity to fall vertically.

'The history of pot-holing can be told in Alum Pot.' Since the history of pot-holing seems to be composed mainly of a long list of people getting stuck upside down in holes, there was no reason to doubt this. Nor was there any doubt that danger, as always, potentiates camaraderie and encourages fraternisation between the social classes. 'Since its beginning pot-holing has been one of those classless sports that has its own dry sense of humour.' The dry sense of humour is most often demonstrated by the merry cheer that goes up from a team of pot-holers when one of their number falls into the water.

The thrill of getting stuck upside-down in Alum Pot is made even more piquant by the rapidity with which the place fills with water. Five minutes after a storm, Alum Pot is on its second rinse. 'A man would be flushed away like a twig.' Imagine what would happen to a twig. But man was not made to cower with his nerve untested. 'There is danger of death', announced the voice-over, 'in jumping off a chair in your own kitchen.' It sounded like a convincing argument until you remembered that nobody with all his marbles spends much time jumping off chairs in his own kitchen.

A plodding but commendable documentary series, *Stalin* (LWT) concluded by admitting that the Stalinist system is still in existence. This was a large concession to reality. If the beginning of the series had been as tough-minded as the end, there would have been at least a hint of the possibility that Stalin was merely developing a repressive apparatus which had been dreamed up and put into action by Lenin. But that would have been too much to hope for. As usual, footage ruled, and most of the footage from the first decade of the Soviet Union shows things being built, not people being broken.

17 September, 1978

Wuthering depths

THE latest but not the best in the Beeb's long line of classic serials, *Wuthering Heights* (BBC2), is the blithering pits.

There is a good case for restoring to the tale some of the romantic tempestuousness it must have generated in the minds of its original readers. But tempestuousness is one thing: a tornado is another. Every time Heathcliff opens his mouth to scream, a geyser of rain hits him in the face.

There is a famous short film by W. C. Fields called *The Fatal Glass of Beer*. Purporting to be in Alaska, Fields establishes this fact by repeatedly going to the door of his cabin, opening it, saying, 'It ain't a fit night out for man nor beast,' and getting hit in the face with a bucket of snow. Perhaps that is what Heathcliff is trying to say. 'It ain't a fit night out for man nor beast, Cathy.' Pfwoosh.

As a reporter, John Pilger usually comes under the heading of blunt but effective, stronger in viewpoint than memorable for phrase. But with *Do You Remember Vietnam?* (ATV) he attained a kind of eloquence. Pilger has got on my nerves in the past and doubtless will again in the future, but this time his gravity and the subject's matched each other. The result was a good programme: unglib, awkward to handle, hard to ignore.

Tom Mangold of the BBC had already been back to Vietnam, so Pilger was obliged to cover some of the same ground, up to and including a tour of the war museum in

Saigon. But he has been reporting Vietnam for most of his adult life, so it was not surprising that what he had to say about what he was seeing carried the implication that he had seen plenty more.

Indeed the most telling image was a blank. Pilger said that he had had the idea at one stage early on of keeping in touch with a Vietnamese family to find out what would happen to them as the war progressed, but one by one the members of the family were killed or just vanished, so that eventually he had to give up. You can't get film of something like that: you have to say it, and Pilger found a way of saying it.

Like Mangold, Pilger evinced a certain amount of worry about what the North Vietnamese might currently be doing to some of the people they had liberated from the Imperialist yoke. The Viet Cong, for example, have disappeared. After doing more than their share of the suffering, they seem to be wielding less than their share of the power. It could be said that Pilger didn't make enough of such anomalies, and that he was too quick to discount the horrors of forced labour by praising the compassion which the conquerors are undoubtedly showing towards the abandoned children of American soldiers.

But on the whole Pilger's message wasn't only clear, it was manifestly correct. If the Americans had stayed out of Vietnam, Vietnam would have stood a better chance of becoming what the Americans wanted it to be. The North Vietnamese never had any intention of being dominated by China. The domino theory was wrong. Millions of innocent people were killed or maimed to no purpose. Unrhetorically and believably, Pilger called this 'the saddest truth of my time'.

There was tape of Kissinger referring to 'occasional difficulties in reaching a final solution'. Like the effects of defoliant, such language still lingers, but plain speech must eventually prevail, if only because Vietnam is no longer a vital issue to anyone except the locals. So they can count their blessings as far as one, at least.

Against my expectations, I enjoyed *No Man's Land* (ATV). Ages ago I had read the text and decided there was not very much in it, but it turns out that one's friends were right when they said – usually at explanatory length – that the piece plays like a dream. It is only a step from conceding that to conceding that form equals content and that the play is therefore a profound work.

Certainly it is an amazingly skilful one. No wonder actors and directors love Pinter. He knows so much about what they would like to do. Actors love drinking on stage. During the course of *No Man's Land* the two leading characters are obliged to imbibe at least a hundred glasses of Scotch each. Meanwhile the two minor characters are required to make exits and entrances. Actors love doing that, too, and directors love telling them when and how. At one point Terence Rigby took almost a minute to go through a door, doing about sixty-five double takes and slow burns.

No Man's Land is like a chess game being played out long after a draw should have been declared, since there are only two knights and two pawns left on the board. As the pawns, Mr Rigby and Michael Kitchen rose voraciously to the opportunities provided by Pinter's scatological dialogue. Actors love such lines because the sting is always in the tail, never in the nose. 'A stitch in time saves nine.' 'What?' 'I said a stitch in time saves nine, scout.' 'I suppose so.' 'You suppose so? You *suppose* so? Did you hear that? He *supposes* so. Listen snot-nose, this is a proverb we're dealing with, not some half-arsed tentative philosophical speculation … ' Something like that, only better.

The two knights, of course, were beyond criticism. They were probably also beyond being convinced that they were mainly engaged in making something out of nearly nothing. Gielgud spoke with superbly dignified seediness, while Richardson did drunken falls that would have taxed the courage of Evel Knievel. No two literary men in history have ever talked less about literature, but it didn't matter.

There was only one moment of real wit. ('Lord Lancer? He's not one of the Bengal Lancers, is he?') Everything else *sounded* like wit. Consisting entirely of its own technique, the play is so decadent that it might as well be called innocent, so sophisticated that it might as well be called naive. I lapped it up with disgust. What a con. And what a gift.

Fearless Frank (BBC2), by Andrew Davies, was a good play about Frank Harris, with Leonard Rossiter rampant in the title role. The discrepancy between fantasy and reality in Harris's love-life was firmly pointed out, although even now the full sordidness of the means by which he attained satisfaction can apparently not be faced. There were no enemas or irrigations on view.

The Italian Marxist composer *Luigi Nono* (BBC2) proclaims the necessity for contemporary music to 'intervene' in something called 'the sonic reality of our time'. Apparently it should do this by being as tuneless as possible. There were shots of Nono's apartments to indicate that he is even better off than the usual run of Italian Marxist composers. There was also footage of his fellow Venetians performing alienated tasks, such as selling fish to one another. The implication was that it would need Nono's music to give such tasks meaning.

It was painfully evident that Nono lacks the mental equipment to take in the suggestion that his job is not to make selling fish as interesting as his music, but to make his music as interesting as selling fish. Among artists without talent Marxism will always be popular, since it enables them to blame society for the fact that nobody wants to hear what they have to say.

8 October, 1978

Wilde and Whistler

A SET of production values in search of a script, *Lillie* (LWT) has a definite appeal for the eye, but goes through the mind like a stream of neutrinos.

So great is the beauty and powerful the talent of Francesca Annis that she almost contrives to distract you from the inanity of the lines she has been given to speak. But always when she is not on the screen, and often enough when she is, you realise that the story being told is not worth telling. On this evidence, Lillie Langtry was no more interesting than any other social-climbing glamour-puss.

In reality, the Jersey Lily was one of those rare women who help to forge the shaky but enduring alliance between high society and the upper reaches of Bohemia — an uneasy symbiosis which is traditionally known under the collective title of the *beau monde*. She fascinated not only the nobs, who are always easily fascinated, but the artists, who in many cases can be fascinated only against their will. She seems to have been a kind of walking poem. That the Prince of Wales went to bed with her means nothing at all: who cares about him? But that she appealed to the imaginations of men like Wilde and Whistler is a fact not without significance, and the proper mainspring of any story about her life.

Wilde and Whistler are in the script all right. Indeed they are rarely out of it. As they arrive, people cry, 'It's Wilde and Whistler!' On they rush like Morecambe and Wise, except that their material is not as good. They are more like Little and Large. The author of the script, David Butler, either has no idea of what the two great wits of their age might have sounded like, or else lacks the wherewithal to evoke it. Instead, Whistler whoofles and Wilde wilts.

Whistler is played as a worldly-wise, twinkling buffer all overcome with fond understanding of Lillie's dilemmas. He is always being wonderful. Wilde is played as a swoopy aesthete. The steel of his repartee is quite missing: everything he says is as soft as his wrist. He is always being even more wonderful than Whistler. Wilde calls Lillie 'Divinity' and goes dewy-eyed with thwarted longing.

Whistler, Wilde and their smart friends have conversations about Lillie while she is off in Rotten Row vamping the quality. These discussions are liberally punctuated with the Period Laugh, which has not been heard on such a scale since *Napoleon in Love* some years back. The Period Laugh is the laugh that starts with N. 'She is ... changing.' 'Nhah-hah-hah-hah!' 'In that way the Sphinx keeps her secrets.' 'Nhergh-hergh-hergh-hergh!' 'I'm not surpri-hi-hi-hised.' 'Nho-ho-ho-ho.' At the end of these exchanges, people say, 'I'll see myself out,' which indicates, for the Victorian era, a strange shortage of butlers.

But even the largest budget is not limitless. The big ball-scenes probably ate up most of the money. During these, Lillie has been introduced to progressively grander grandees. At the climactic moment of each episode, she has sunk to one knee and risen saying 'Your Grace' or 'Your Highness', filling the screen with an enigmatic half-smile as the titles roll.

Now at last she has met the Prince of Wales. 'We have been fools', he murmurs through his beard, 'to have waited so long.' But the possibility that she might have gone on waiting longer, or even indefinitely, is not even considered. The script seems to regard her affair with the Prince as inevitable. There is nothing to distinguish Lillie's values from those of her status-mad maid. 'Next to 'eem, all zee arzers are nussing.'

This Lillie Langtry is a power-groupie. Such women can still be found today. Their chief ambition in life is to sit next to Henry Kissinger. Perhaps the real Lillie Langtry was like that too. But even if she was, she aroused in some very talented people that peculiar sense, half exaltation and half heart-break, which comes from knowing a woman so beauti-ful that she is like a work of art. If anybody could impersonate such a woman, Francesca Annis could, but not even she can do it without lines.

29 October, 1978

Voyage of the Beagle

JUST in time to boost the Beeb's morale, *The Voyage of Charles Darwin* (BBC2) looks certain, on the strength of its first episode, to be a raging success.

Reputedly a million pounds has been laid out, much of it on constructing a practical replica of the *Beagle*. For once the money looks well spent. One of the many symptoms of the severe case of the jitters which the BBC has been suffering in recent years is the way the *Radio Times* has tended to sprout articles in which it is explained that James Burke has been sent to 473 different countries in search of the connecting link between Tutankhamun's jock-strap and the modern vacuum cleaner, or that Sue Lawley has been paid large amounts of money in order to stop reading things out in one studio and start reading things out in another. Such revelations sound like money thrown to the winds, and sort ill with further revelations that money is what the BBC is short of.

But *Charles Darwin* is a blockbuster that looks like working. Here is an indication of what a BBC department can still do when it has the proper amount of money to spend. If all the other departments were in the same position, the BBC would be strong again within a matter of months. For one thing, competent personnel would stop gravitating towards ITV. All that is required is a decent-sized licence fee, preferably collectable at the TV set's point of sale. At the moment, the Corporation is forced to demand its money with menaces. It is ludicrous that the broadcasting system which is still very properly the envy of all the world should be reduced to sending snooper vans in search of defaulting subscribers.

As to Darwin himself, he is played by Malcolm Stoddard, an engaging actor who is just right for the role, since he has brains as well as beauty, and has lately learned not to detract from the latter by baring his bottom teeth. Darwin comes equipped with a misunderstanding father who complains about his good-for-nothing son 'cluttering the room with all manner of dead insects'. Declining, after a glimpse of what passes for surgery at the time, to become a surgeon like his father, Charles goes up to Cambridge to do a bit more of being good for nothing. Cambridge, like all the other locations, is photographed with a faultless eye for period and atmosphere.

Finally it is time to join Fitzroy on the *Beagle*, but only after father has had a chance to say: 'The whole wild scheme is out of the question.' The lines might be clichés, but the passions underlying them are not. You can feel Darwin's scientific curiosity growing hotter like the rising sun. A real ship on a real ocean, the *Beagle* puts to sea. For the next three years Fitzroy and Darwin will be sublimating themselves towards immortality. In a voice-over, Darwin calls the voyage in prospect 'the very essence of excitement and adventure'. He is perfectly right.

In *World Gymnastics* (BBC1), Ronda Schwandt of the US was on the beam when Alan Weeks had yet another of his Great Moments in the History of Commentating. 'Whichever way you look at it,' burbled Alan, 'the improvement by the Americans is really quite AAGH!' While Alan had been talking, Ronda had mistimed a somersault and landed sensationally astraddle the beam, thereby sustaining a shattering impact to her defenceless bracket. Despite what must have been a barely tolerable amount of pain and shock, within the regulation ten seconds Ronda was back in action. So, of course, was Alan.

The gymnastics championships were screened by both the

BBC and ITV – a pointless duplication, except that it gave her fans twice as many chances to see just how beautiful Nadia Comaneci has become. The commentators encouraged us to look upon it as a tragedy that her new shapeliness has inhibited her old agility. But I, for one, can't say that I mind. There is something dreadful about those undernourished and over-flexible little girls that the Russians and Romanians field a new batch of every year.

It is a matter of some satisfaction that Nadia can no longer do the sinister little stand-up curtsey with which the pre-pubescent girl gymnasts indicate that they are ready for their next death-defying routine. Saluting with upraised pelican wings, a curved spine and tiny buttocks thrust rearward, they erupt into a flurry of movements that you really don't much want to see.

Some of this year's tricks look outright dangerous. Filatova, doing a double flick-flack plus twisting somersault dismount from the beam, missed her footing on the second flick-flack and landed on her neck. An inch either way and she could have been dead. Of the Russian girls, only the sweetly fluent Mukhina harks back to the days when the Soviet Union produced gymnasts more like ballerinas than like bullets.

5 November, 1978

Blood and guts

HALF satisfying and half frustrating, the first episode of Jonathan Miller's *The Body in Question* (BBC2) left you hungry for more in some respects and in others shouting for less.

Paradoxically it was in the blood-and-guts department that the programme was at its most gripping. Dressed in his dissection outfit, Miller stood benevolently alert behind a table piled with human offal. Leavening scientific inquiry with nervous humour, he combined the roles of Vesalius in Padua and Hawkeye Pierce in Korea. Meanwhile the assembled organs played dead, but it emerged through various hints that they had once been the insides of a lady of a certain age. Or anyway I think it was a lady – sometimes when I had my hands over my eyes my fingers got in my ears.

Apart from the inevitable soot-stains in the lungs, the subject seemed to have departed this life in reasonable shape. Grasping an appropriate tool, Miller picked up the heart and made a power-dive into the left ventricle. Fantastic Voyage! 'It's years since I've done this,' said Miller reassuringly. He wasn't being reassuring about what might happen if he did the same to you. He was being reassuring about his own talents, which we might think were superhuman unless he reminded us occasionally that even he sometimes forgets what he has learned.

The gall bladder disgorged bile. The bile was supposed to be green, but on the screen it looked dark blue. Either the organ's owner had been a Martian or my set was out of whack. The latter possibility seemed more likely, since recently Frank Bough had been looking like Joshua Nkomo. While I thus mused, Miller was turning his attention to the liver. It was immediately clear that the liver was to be the star turn. It was large, plump and full of potential, like a whoopee cushion. Miller sliced into it. It looked remarkably healthy. In fact it looked good enough to ... wait a second.

Cutting up dead meat according to traditional procedures, Miller was obliged to keep things simple. Having to hold knives kept his hands still. But after doffing his apron he was free to argue. The explanatory hands were back in action, swooping all over the screen like a manic pilot recounting a dog-fight. 'Being embodied is the only intelligible way of being personified,' Miller explained – a viewpoint lent force by the fact that its proponent is as embodied as they come.

Wearing a wide-angle lens, the camera sat face to face with the sage's embodied personification while it filled the air with fingers a foot long.

Unfortunately the arguments themselves were often insubstantial. Miller has a poet's gift of metaphor: he is marvellous at seeing similarities. He also has the poet's tendency to mistake a metaphor for a rigorously considered proposition. Wittgenstein said that we should not be seduced by language. Miller has been seduced even by Wittgenstein.

What do we mean, Miller asked, when we say that we have a stabbing pain? It was exactly the kind of awkward question that Wittgenstein was always putting. Miller asked a policeman who had been stabbed what it had felt like. The policeman said that it had felt like being hit with a cricket bat. Miller retired satisfied, supposing his point made. But Wittgenstein would have asked the policeman what he thought being hit with a cricket bat felt like.

Miller can't help seeming to toy with ideas, since he is incapable of ignoring any of them. T. S. Eliot said that Henry James had a mind so fine no idea could violate it. Few bees are unable to find at least a temporary welcome in Miller's bonnet. Miller is justifiably outraged by the narrowness of modern specialisation. He is convinced that all the intellectual adventures, whether scientific or artistic, are essentially the same adventure. This conviction is both true and valuable. We are very lucky that so brilliantly energetic a man exists to hold it. But there is also such a thing as being a prisoner of your own versatility.

It has been said that Miller is a Renaissance man. Certainly he has the gifts. But really it was intensity of effort, rather than universality of range, that characterised the men of the Renaissance. Even at their most fiercely competitive they were ready to leave some departments of knowledge and achievement to be taken care of by others. Leonardo was a throwback to a previous age. Unable to resist a challenge, he carved in ice and painted his greatest masterpiece on a wet wall, where it has been crumbling ever since – a lasting, although not alas permanent, warning to every genius in a hurry.

Genius in its cups was the subject of *Dylan* (BBC2), a two-hour dramatised examination of Dylan Thomas's death throes. Remarkably poised for a work devoted to this particular subject, it was all the more frightening for that. Ronald Lacey turned in a bravura performance composed largely of sweating, hawking, spitting, lurching, dry-retching, dribbling and falling down. Somehow he managed to convey a central dignity holding the whole mess together. At the end it didn't seem entirely impossible that a woman looking like Gayle Hunnicutt would be on hand so that he could die in her arms.

Miss Hunnicutt grows more subtle with each performance. She found a hundred ways of looking quietly desperate while Dylan roamed in blind search of a booze-filled teat. She looked in love with what he had been and in some sense was still, even though the man on show was a perambulating disaster. The programme rang with the passing bell and the poet's thrilling voice. Mr Lacey did a good enough imitation of the latter to make it seem credible when the student audiences were shown to be in ecstasies as he recited 'Fern Hill'.

Scripted by Simon Raven and introduced by a Wodehouse-Playhouse title sequence, the first episode of *Edward and Mrs Simpson* (Thames) had a jaunty air. A beautifully dressed production with all the right clothes, cars and locations, it is already suffering slightly from the fact that Edward Fox has too formidable a presence to be quite believable as a Weak King. Fox's great gift, steadily becoming more pronounced as he matures, is to body forth hidden depths. All Edward ever had was hidden shallows.

Still, Fox gives the role all it can take, if not all he's got. He makes with the flared nostril, the flexed upper lip and the mellow bellow. Cynthia Harris looks just right as the lady who did us all such a favour by separating Edward from his throne. It is hard to tell whether she is acting badly or else giving a very good impersonation of the kind of American woman who sounds like a bad actress.

12 November, 1978

Howareowebees

SEMI-INTELLIGIBLE in five different languages, Sacha Distel was just the man to host *Miss World* (BBC1), a contest which he had every right to call a voyazh of discarvry.

This year even more than in most previous years, the salient challenge proposed by the voyazh of discarvry was to discarvre among the contestants a girl you would bother to look twice at in the street. The smart money was on Miss Mexico, who had a fetching smile. But of Sacha's five languages she seemed to misunderstand him in three, one of them her own. Her subsequent confusion probably did her no good at all with the judges – a panel of intellectual giants which included the lead singer of Thin Lizzy.

When Sacha asks a girl if she has any howareowebees, he is really asking her if she has any hobbies, but she would need to have known him for a long time if she were to rumble this straight away. Those girls with English as a native language usually ignored Sacha and addressed themselves straight to camera, placing due emphasis on their philanthropic activities. My compatriot Miss Australia was outstanding in this department. Her main howareowebee, it transpired, was visiting the aged. She loved old people. She had known a man who was eighty-four years old, but he had died.

As usual, the show's main area of purely visual interest was not near the end, when the few finalists were clumping around being interviewed, but near the start, when all the girls in the contest came lurching forward one at a time in national dress. Thus we discarvred that the national dress of Malta, for example, is a coal sack. But the climax was rich with drama, even if it was short of personnel. Of the seven girls left in, Miss Mexico certainly did not expect to finish as low as fourth. Her smile at hearing the news was the bravest of her life.

Miss Argentina, on the other hand, was certainly not expecting to win. She reacted as if tragedy had struck. Did she face death from some radical group if she finished higher than third? Perhaps it was just all too much for her. Certainly there is something about the way Sacha sings that makes a girl feel life has no more to offer. Beside herself under her crown of tinsel, Miss Argentina cried as if her tiny heart would break. The star filters in the cameras turned her cataracts of tears into nebulae.

At the moment television in the evening is like an Open University extension course in the sciences. Top-rating lecturer is undoubtedly David Bellamy, otherwise known as *Botanic Man* (Thames). Bellamy's enthusiasm has a lot to make up for. To start with, there is his beard. He also has an extraordinary manner of speaking, in which one impediment is piled on top of another. But it can't be denied that he generates excitement when he appears abruptly from among the mangroves and starts poking frogs at you.

'Vese are Hamilton fwogs,' he announces, holding a Hamilton fwog. The Hamilton fwog looks at Bellamy as a fwog might do if, after a blameless lifetime in the mud, it were suddenly to find itself an international celebrity. Undeterred, Bellamy raves on, explaining that Hamilton fwogs possess special skins 'fwew which vey bweave'. Thus the Hamilton fwog is able to survive and not become one of the 'mere memowies of pahst ages of evowution'.

Meanwhile, back at *The Voyage of Charles Darwin* (BBC2), the theory of evolution is an increasingly noticeable glimmer in the hero's eye. Like Bellamy, Darwin has a beard, but it is a different shape, allowing him to speak more clearly. Happily naming mountains after each other, Darwin and Fitzroy are currently sailing up and down the coast of Patagonia. Something of a nutter, Fitzroy has been trying to convert the locals. But Darwin is occupied with something even holier – the quest for understanding.

One of the many strengths of this marvellous series is that it knows how to give dramatic force to such elementary propositions. You really feel, when Darwin starts digging up bones on the beach, that he is engaged on a sacred quest. Slowly the prehistoric skeleton takes shape. Is it Plasterkasterops? Is it Proposaurus Rex? No, it is a perfectly believable-looking ancient beast. The production values are consistently high. There have been some unconvincing natives jumping up and down shouting 'Boola boola', but doubtless the original tribe likewise jumped up and down shouting 'Boola boola', while Fitzroy said things like: 'My God, Darwin, these fellows look unconvincing.'

In the second episode of *The Body in Question* (BBC2), Jonathan Miller cut back on the philosophising and got to grips with his subject, which in this case was a pain in the guts. How to diagnose it? Tricks of the trade were revealed. I was stunned to hear that a certain kind of pain which has haunted a friend of mine for years, and which has defied the diagnostic skills of numerous physicians, is in fact one of the elementary sure-fire signs of kidney trouble. This made me wonder how many tricks of the trade the trade was actually in possession of. Do all those doctors out there know what Miller knows, and if not why not?

Anyway, the camera once again went inside the large intestine to watch peristalsis taking place. The gut contracting and dilating reminded me of something. I button-punched to the *News* on BBC1 and found the Prime Minister making a speech about the necessity to go on curbing inflation. The way his mouth contracted and dilated reminded me of something. Button-punching back to *The Body in Question* I suddenly found that everything had become clear. There is a close resemblance between the mouth and the large intestine at those moments when they are both in the process of manufacturing the same stuff. I had made what James Burke would call a Connection.

One has been kept from previous series of *Some Mothers Do 'Ave 'Em* (BBC1) by its awful title, but it is time to say what everybody else is saying – that the show is a must. Largely due to Michael Crawford's pertinacity in setting up his stunts and special effects, the slapstick is almost invariably funny. The level of language is high, too. 'Did it have to come to this? Ejaculated from our fixed abode.' It is fitting that a hero so maladroit should be a Malaprop as well. The central character is so consistently developed that the audience take it for granted the house will fall down only a few weeks after he has started to live in it.

The Queen Mother attended the *Royal Variety Performance* (BBC1). She also once volunteered to be bombed by the Luftwaffe, but that was some time ago, and perhaps nowadays she should be more careful about exposing her august and beloved person to mechanised outrage. David Jacobs recited a poem in her honour. Miserably composed, it referred to 'a Scottish larse'. I tuned out when a rabbit in a red spangled suit started playing the piano.

19 November, 1978

Dr Beckman's apparatus

HIBERNATION was the subject of a *Horizon* (BBC2) called *The Big Sleep*. If waking up had been the subject the programme would probably have been called 'For Whom The Bell Tolls'.

In the Land of the Media, the habit of pinching famous

titles is by now firmly ingrained. There was a time when media people made at least an attempt at originality, straining their tiny imaginations to produce variants of *The Loneliness of the Long Distance Runner* and *Have Gun, Will Travel*. An article or a programme would be called 'The Loneliness of the Long Distance Telephone Operator' or 'Have Eggs Will Omelette'. It was dull, but it wasn't outright theft. Calling a programme on hibernation *The Big Sleep* is outright theft.

The level of invention having revealed itself to be so low, it was not surprising that the moral sense was low as well. The programme asked no questions about the ethics of what the scientists were up to. It did not even seem to be aware that questions of ethics might be raised. It just nodded its silly head admiringly while the men in the white coats got on with the job.

Animals, it appears, have been helping us in our attempts to understand hibernation. 'A sedated catheter', crooned the soothing voice-over, 'is inserted into the sleeping bear's bladder.' Presumably the voice-over meant that it was the bear that would not feel the catheter, and not the catheter that would not feel the bear. This was by no means an easy presumption, however, considering what has been happening to other animals. Not only have bears been helping us. Squirrels and rats have been helping us too.

Dr Beckman was shown experimenting on a squirrel, whose entire brain was exposed to view under a transparent cap. 'The animal has had the top of its skull surgically replaced', murmured the voice-over, 'so that it can be clamped firmly into Beckman's apparatus.' One's plans to clamp Dr Beckman into an apparatus of one's own devising were interrupted by an assurance that 'there are no nerves in the brain itself.' This was a relief. It was safe to assume, then, that the squirrel did not mind the experiment at all. Later on it could always wear a little beret.

Dr Swan operated on a rat. In my notes it says that Dr Rat

operated on swan, but I'm afraid I was merely doodling to get my eyes off the screen. 'Swan', breathed the ever-attentive voice-over, 'is about to lift the still beating heart out of a decapitated rat.' After Swan had accomplished this feat, he clamped the still beating heart into his apparatus. 'The rat heart continues to beat for three hours.' We were assured that the research was so important that Dr Swan has devoted his life to it. Elsewhere in the laboratory, the rat's head was no doubt moved to hear this.

About ten years back a craze developed among the psycho-logists for studying something called REM sleep. Your eye-balls move when you dream. The psychologists used up a lot of animals while examining the implications of this fact. What the psychologists found out from the animals was nothing beside what the animals found out from the psychologists. The cats, in particular, found out that the average psycho-logist is capable of practically anything. In reputable Ameri-can universities cats were kept awake indefinitely by being made to stand on bricks surrounded by water.

The results yielded by this kind of research might or might not be useful, but there can be no doubt about the usefulness of what we learn about the researchers. Protected by the otherwise valuable conventions of free inquiry, a scientist is armed even against the disapproval of his own colleagues. If he is a butcher – and the less original he is, the more likely he is to be cruel – there is nothing to stop him except the laws of the land. It follows inexorably that if the laws of the land change, the pretensions of scientific research change with them. Whatever is not forbidden will be done.

In a *World in Action* (Granada) called *The Hunt for Dr Mengele* (happily it was not called either 'The Loneliness of the Long Distance Nutter' or 'Have False Passport, Will Hide Out in South America') there were films and stills from the concentration camps to show what Nazi scientific research was like. A law unto himself in Auschwitz, Josef Mengele had a marvellous opportunity to prove scientifically that the Jews were an inferior breed. He particularly favoured experiments on twin children, since one child could be preserved as a control while the other was cut up, often alive.

There is no reason to suppose that Mengele was particularly nuts. Within recent years, government research funds in this country have been used to prove, among other things, that a cat with a severed spinal column will have trouble landing on its feet when dropped from a certain height. How can we be sure that a man capable of doing such a thing to a cat would not do the same sort of thing to a human being if he were allowed to? How can *he* be sure? The true villains are the men who do the allowing. Unfortunately most of the Nazi hierarchs cheated justice. Which does not mean, of course, that their devoted minions should be allowed to cheat it as well.

So far Mengele has got away with it. He is holed up snugly in Paraguay, protected by that country's obscene government and by his own financial resources. On the strength of this programme, the greatest danger he runs is of being bored to death by his terrible friends. *World in Action* took a lot of risks but were scarcely likely to succeed where the Israeli agents had failed.

In *The World About Us* (BBC2) the astonishing Clare Francis sailed around the world. She was lucky in being able to film her own achievement. Poor Schubert has had to rely on his admirers, with results exemplified by *A Winter's Journey* (BBC2), one of the worst arts programmes I have ever seen. A little classic of misinformation, it conveyed the impression that Schubert was a tragic, doomed rebel 'against the bourgeois world'. He was, on the contrary, bourgeois to the roots and a byword for merriment. That lager commercial – the one in which Schubert is tempted off to the pub, leaving his symphony unfinished – seemed a probing analysis by comparison.

'Do you think I'm sex?' sang Rod Stewart on *Top of the Pops* (BBC1). In the course of time it became clear, or at any rate less unclear, that this was Rod's way of asking whether we thought he was sexy. Unless we thought he was sex, he would not be hap, and would eventually go craze.

26 November, 1978

Jean-Paul Kean

IRIS MURDOCH and other professional students of the mighty French savant would no doubt decline to back me up, but speaking as a highly unqualified layman I feel bound to assert that Jean-Paul Sartre has only ever had one real idea in his life.

The idea is enshrined in his first little book on existentialism. It is the idea that our lives are something we can make and remake for ourselves from day to day. I have always had the impression that the idea came to him when he was sitting one evening – or afternoon or even morning, it would have made no difference – in the stygian depths of a Left Bank club. On a little stage, Juliette Greco was singing. At another table, Simone de Beauvoir was writing in a very large notebook. Sartre had one eye on each of them. *Tiens*, it was a long time ago.

Be that as it may, the idea, or notion, is surely the driving force of Sartre's play *Kean*, which last weekend was given to us as the *Play of the Month* on BBC1, in a translation by Frank Hauser. Slap-happily composed but full of interest, the piece came springing to life with a zest that made you wonder how a man capable of raising Kean from the dead should have been so concerned, at a later stage of his career, to bury Flaubert beyond hope of recovery. The answer, I think, is that Sartre, like Camus, simply admired and envied actors. Actors are, after all, the only true existentialists. Or so writers tend to believe.

As evoked by Sartre, Kean is an actor whose own life is his greatest role. Inspired by debt like Balzac, jumping in and out of fancy dressing-gowns like Wagner, Sartre's Kean lives the life of an aristocrat at a time when actors are still not admitted into polite society or even into hallowed ground. The first exponent of Sartre's title role was the great Pierre Brasseur, who can be seen playing a different, humbler version of the same sort of character in *Les Enfants du Paradis*. In this production the eponymous hero was Anthony Hopkins, who seized his opportunity with both hands, threw it across the room, picked it up again, throttled it, wrestled it to the floor and knelt panting on its chest.

Hopkins did a more than passable Great Actor number. Largely it consisted of saying some parts of a given sentence-veryquicklyand oth-ers ver-y slow-ly, while jazzing up the dynamics with the occasional RANDOM SHOUT. Meanwhile he was moving all over the split-level set in perpetual search of a resting place for his irrepressible spirit, etc. Bloodshot eyes and a bad shave completed the picture of boiling genius. Hopkins kept it up for two hours and obviously could have gone on for a week.

Robert Stephens impersonated the Prince of Wales. This gave him a chance to wear satin breeches and make with one of his specialities, the Big Laugh. The Big Laugh goes 'Mwah-hah-hah-hargh!' The Prince of Wales was fascinated with Kean. So was all society. Was he below them or above them? 'He's beginning to intrigue me, this seducer,' said one. 'Wha-ha-ha-hat no-ho-ho-honsense,' said another, meaning, 'What nonsense.'

All reacted severally when the footman announced Mr Kean. 'Kean?' '*Kean?*' 'KEAN?' It was clumsy enough dramatically. But the sense of adventure was in it. The would-be brisk exchanges and the long-winded speeches were alike energised by the central boldness of the conception. The artist making his own way according to his own rules – years ago, when his imagination was young, Sartre lit up at that idea. It just goes to show that even genius can sometimes be touched by talent.

Edward and Mrs Simpson (Thames) would be unbelievable if it were not so believable, and vice versa. Edward Fox is too interesting to be credible as Edward VIII, who by all objective accounts was boring beyond description. Yet the series easily overcomes the handicap of this fundamental improbability. Simon Raven has given Warris Hussein the kind of script directors dream of. Mr Hussein, one hazards, is grateful, since in his time he has had to deal with the kind of script directors have nightmares about. Remember Chopin and George Sand? Mr Hussein could make little of their intelligence. Out of Edward VIII's and Mrs Simpson's consuming dumbness he is able to make much. The difference is in the writing.

It is still not certain whether the actress acting Mrs Simpson can actually act. But she can do a good imitation of that terrible sleep-walking look that you see on the faces of ladies bent on getting married to destiny. There is no doubt, of course, about which actress in the series best embodies the historical sensitivity of the whole enterprise. As Queen Mary, Dame Peggy Ashcroft is quietly giving everyone else on television a lesson in how to act for the camera. Since she so rarely acts for the camera, the secret of her astonishing command must lie not in a specialised training, but in a general ability to accept, employ and transcend any set of technical limitations imposed on her. Dame Peggy is a bit of all right.

Charlie's Angels (ITV) spent the week at a health farm for women. The health farm was swarming with pretty bodies, but the Angels were prettier. The decor of the health farm was pink. Pink track-suits, pink towels, pink everything – the whole layout was specifically designed to flood your picture with pink splodge. Chris (Cheryl Ladd) wore pink shorts, out of which the pert cheeks of her delectable bottom hung a precisely calculated half an inch.

As the atmosphere throbbed with libido, dykey female heavies closed in on the Angels. The lesbians were after Chris! Perspiring prettily in a sauna, Chris didn't notice the hairy hand of the diesel masseuse as it locked the door and turned up the heat. Still firmly wrapped in her pink towel, Chris flaked. Finally the Sapphists stretched her out on a massage table and started steaming her to death with hot towels. The other two Angels burst in and removed every towel except the last. Sigh.

3 December, 1978

Island of the stud tortoises

IN the continuously astonishing *Voyage of Charles Darwin* (BBC1), a couple of hundred thousand giant lizards, few of them members of Equity, have been doing walk-ons, or rather glide-ons.

For the animals, birds and fish of the Galapagos Islands, where not a lot happens, the arrival of the Beeb's film unit must have been the biggest event since Darwin himself made the scene. No wonder, then, that they have shown themselves to be such keen performers. Out of the dressing room and on to the set in less time than it takes the assistant director to lift his loud-hailer, they are ready to fight, run, fly, dive, eat, drink and make love without a single tea-break. Apart from one iguana who looks a bit like Corin Redgrave, there is not a trouble-maker in sight.

A rape scene starring two giant tortoises, one of each sex, was particularly effective. Perhaps objecting to the male's unduly abrupt style of courtship, the female zoomed away at top speed, which looked to be something like a mile a week. Not to be thwarted, the male, who had the general bearing of a Playboy Club key-holder, howled off in pursuit.

It was the work of an epoch for the male to close the gap, but eventually he caught the female. His next task was to mount her. After about an era they were in business, like two Minis one on top of the other. The actor playing Darwin looked on enthralled, just as Darwin must have looked on enthralled – perhaps at the same pair of tortoises, since they live a long time.

Little on the Galapagos Islands has changed. The simple, powerful idea which made possible this most wonderful of all nature series was exactly that – that nothing in these places had changed, and that all you had to do was go there. Another powerful idea was to use Darwin's clear and rhythmic prose to link the narrative. Such inspired notions seem easy to hindsight, yet they spring from the rarest kind of creative imagination. A vast amount of painstaking generalship has gone into the details of this great production, but the secret of its success lies in that first, impossibly ambitious supposition of what might be possible. The BBC has every right to be proud.

Whether the BBC will get a chance to be proud of its Shakespeare enterprise is more doubtful. Destined to come up with brand new productions of all the Shakespeare plays over the next six years, the Bardathon got under way with *Romeo and Juliet* (BBC2). Since the Zeffirelli movie of the same play still stands, with all its faults, as one of the most satisfactory filmed realisations of a Shakespeare text, it might have been smarter to start with something else, and thereby avoid comparisons.

Verona seemed to have been built on very level ground, like the floor of a television studio. The fact that this artificiality was half accepted and half denied told you that you were not in Verona at all, but in that semi-abstract, semi-concrete, wholly uninteresting city which is known to students as Messina, after the producer of the same name. A glance at the credits in *Radio Times* confirmed the suspicion that Cedric Messina was indeed the man in charge, but this did not mean that the director, Alvin Rakoff, would be entirely without responsibility. Indeed it soon became clear that Messrs Messina and Rakoff were made for each other.

The Trevor Nunn production of *Antony and Cleopatra* should have shown everybody that the way to get the effect of wealth with a television budget is to shoot tight on the actors; use a few good props; and keep the background darkly suggestive. But in Messina the lesson was never learned. So here once again was the supposedly teeming street life, composed of an insufficient number of extras dutifully teeming as hard as they could. All the perspectives were evenly lit, as if specifically to reveal their poverty of detail. The eye went hungry, which made the ear ravenous.

Unfortunately there was not much worth listening to. As the Chorus, Gielgud set standards of speaking which none of the youngsters in the cast could even begin to match. In his opening fourteen lines he showed how the pentameter needs to be both analysed and integrated, so that its formality and its freedom are alike revealed. 'From forth the fatal loins of these two foes/A pair of star-cross'd lovers take their life ... ' Ten beats, five in each line, with the line break barely observed but definitely not missed, and the word 'lovers' picked out at the zenith of the rhythmic curve. All it takes is talent and application. In 1935 Gielgud played Romeo opposite Ashcroft's Juliet. Imagine how terrific they must have been.

Anyway, Patrick Ryecart and Rebecca Saire looked fetching enough in the title roles. Both spoke cleanly, but neither gave the sense of having spotted the difference between prose and blank verse. They didn't murder the poetry: they merely ignored it. In the long run Mercutio's approach was preferable. He *did* murder it, breaking every line up into tiny, twitching pieces. 'O, then. I see. Queen Mab. Hath been. With you.' He was. Enough. To drive. You mad, but at least he had the virtue of demonstrating, by getting it so wrong, that Shakespeare's verse is something that has to be got right.

The first in LWT's new series of Alan Bennett plays, *Me*,

I'm Afraid of Virginia Woolf, was one word too long in its title but otherwise perfectly judged. 'In the entire history of the world,' said the author on voice-over, 'Hopkins could recall no one of note who had been called Trevor.' The scene was Halifax, where it was Trevor's fate to conduct doomed night-school seminars about Bloomsbury and put up with his mother, who relentlessly talked the kind of banalities which Bennett overhears in bus shelters and writes down in his famous notebooks.

'Course *I'd* have been educated if I'd stopped on at school,' observed Trevor's mam. Trevor had no response except to disintegrate even further, showering himself with dandruff. A terrible girlfriend loomed. He fell in love with a male student. On the blackboard, Virginia Woolf's fastidious pro-file was like a signal arriving from a star long dead. Stephen Frears directed with his usual sure touch.

In New York briefly last week, I turned on the television when I woke up and found Nixon talking at the Oxford Union. My sleepy puzzlement about how I had managed to go there in order to watch him talking here was dispelled by a sudden, glowing rage at the effrontery of the man. He clearly imagines himself to be on the come-back trail. Luckily for the country whose constitution he subverted, he seems to be little better now than previously at choosing his allies. With Lord Longford helping him, he has no chance.

10 December, 1978

The flying feet of Frankie Foo

NEVER since Damocles danced beneath the sword has there been anything like the *World Disco Dancing Championships* (Thames), brought to you live from the ravishing Empire Ballroom, Leicester Square.

Disc jockey David Hamilton was the man in charge, his old young features more than usually agog with excitement. According to statistics, he informed us, the audience for this 'greatest dance contest ever held' would be approximately 200,000,000 people around the world. 'Staggering, isn't it? My bottle's gone, I can tell you.' Since David never does much except stand there looking keen, it was hard to see how his performance would be significantly impaired by the defection of his bottle, but that was by the way. Because already it was time to meet what the *TV Times* had courageously billed as 'a celebrity panel of judges'.

Perhaps they were celebrities in the narrowly specialised field of disco dance contest judging. For the general viewer their names tended not to ring a bell, except in the case of Agape Stassinopoulos, Arianna's sister. Agape was described by David as 'the lovely actress from Greece'. Her fair presence was some consolation for the absence of Arianna, who was probably writing a new book that night. The other judges mainly fell into the category of 'international cabaret star'. If you have spent six weeks in a sequinned jacket singing 'My Way' to an audience of uncomprehending Lebanese, you are an international cabaret star.

Most of the dancers were international too. The Australian representative for example, was called Alfonso Falcone. This aroused the expectation that the Italian representative might be called Wokka Whitlam, but before you could say Jack Robinson (of Malawi) on came Frankie Foo from Kuala Lumpur. As the floor pulsed with light and the air shook to the sledgehammer beat, one dancer after another gallantly attempted the impossible task of shaking off his own pudenda without touching them. The athleticism involved was awe-inspiring. Tadyaki Dan of Japan spent most of his time in mid-air, upside down with his hands behind his back, trying to bite pieces out of the floor.

Disco dancing is really dancing for people who hate dancing, since the beat is so monotonous that only the champions can find interesting ways of reacting to it. There is no syncopation, just the steady thump of a giant moron knocking in an endless nail. But with that proviso, this was still an event from which it was difficult to prise loose your attention. Which dancer would have the first hernia of the contest? Would Thomas Brown of Bermuda ('He's a trainee chef! Trace of the old hot stuff there') manage to pull his toes out of his ears before he hit the floor? After the celebrity panel of judges finished totting up the scores, it was Tadyaki Dan of Japan who drove away the TR7 full of money. Doubtless he will be back again next year. So will they all. So will I and the other 199,999,999 viewers.

For a mercy, the Bavarian State Opera's rendition of *Lohengrin* (BBC2) was relatively free from symbolist pretensions. It was just as boring as every other production of *Lohengrin* I have ever seen, but that was inevitable, because *Lohengrin* simply happens to be a bore. The important thing is that it was not *offensively* boring. No Marxist half-wit of a producer equipped the grail knight with a homburg hat. Instead the radiant hero was properly attired in shining armour. His long aluminium combat jacket made his legs look like a hamster's, but at least he wasn't riding a penny-farthing.

Unfortunately he wasn't riding a swan either. Instead of the large aquatic fowl which Wagner was unreasonable enough to specify in the text, the producer had fixed Lohengrin up with alternative means of transport. It took the form of an angel with prop wings. In view of this fact it was strange to hear Lohengrin singing 'Farewell my beloved swan' when he should have been singing 'Farewell my beloved walk-on in tatty angel's costume plus lighting effects.'

The excellence of *Richard II* (BBC1) made it seem doubly strange that so mediocre a production of *Romeo and Juliet* had been chosen to usher in the Bardathon. Why not set the expected standard with something good instead of something bad? Or can't the man in charge tell the difference? Anyway

Richard II had everything that *Romeo and Juliet* hadn't. David Giles was the director. He showed his firm hand immediately, framing the actors' faces as closely as possible while they got on with the essential task of speaking the text.

Whenever the shot loosened, it was in order to view rich costumes, solid props and dense, convincing backgrounds. Thus was fulfilled the first condition of a successful Shakespeare production on television — that it shall not try to look like a movie. The focus must, and should, be on the actors. If there is a vista to be described, let the actor's face describe it with a look. Usually there will be some lines available to help the evocation.

In this production there was fine acting to be had. Derek Jacobi gave intelligent, fastidiously articulated readings from beginning to end. The 'sad stories' soliloquy was as masterfully worked out in the reciting as it was meticulously planned in the shooting, with each turn of thought given its appropriate vocal weight by the actor and its perfectly judged close-up by the director. This kind of technical command is rarely noticed by critics and never by the public, but it is the heart and soul of what makes television drama dramatic.

Jacobi's Richard had let his divinity run away with him. It was a fruitful emphasis to make. In Richard Cottrell's famous stage production Ian McKellen made Richard a tearaway gay. That performance launched McKellen in every sense, including the literal: even for his curtain calls he leapt into position. Jacobi was faced with a hard task in transferring the focus from the physique to the mentality. He did it, though. Not only did he contrive to make you not think of McKellen's Richard, he also managed to make you not think of Jacobi's Claudius. This latter challenge was probably the more important to him.

The revelation of the evening, however, was Jon Finch's Bolingbroke. Finch gave the role the performance it needs, since when you look at the text you see that there is not an awful lot there. Indeed there is a good case for asking the actor playing Bolingbroke to content himself with standing around looking worthily staunch. If he is to do more than that, he must play the role on two levels, speaking what is set down for him and transmitting his ambitions – if it is supposed that they exist – by other means. Finch was adept at finding means. Even when he was standing still you could tell he was heading for the throne of England by the direct route.

17 December, 1978

Underneath her wimple

As usual most of the Christmas humour on television was no funnier than a boil in the nose. On the other hand there were some diverting films on offer, chief among which was *The Sound of Music* (BBC1), the famous epic about an Austrian singing family who sang even the Nazis into submission.

It appears from the titles that the film was made 'with the partial use of ideas by George Hurdalek'. The film stars Julie Andrews as a drop-out nun. Presumably George Hurdalek's original idea was that she should be a drop-out nun with webbed feet, but they used only part of it. 'Underneath her wimple she has curlers in her hair,' sing the other nuns, shaking their heads with amused compassion. This is a partial use of George Hurdalek's original idea, in which she was to have a whole hairdryer under her wimple, with a cable plugged into the refectory wall.

'How do you hold a moonbeam in your hand?' sing the nuns with quizzical adoration, all unaware that the audience is singing a different question, to wit: is the Mother Superior being played by Charles Bronson? Finally Julie packs her bags and splits, joining up with Christopher Plummer, who impersonates a widowed noble naval captain with seven children – a partial use of George Hurdalek's original idea, in which the same character was to be a widowed noble naval captain, juggler and organic chemist with twenty-eight children and a string of polo ponies.

'The sky was so blew today,' over-enunciates Julie, sick with love. Christopher loves her in return, but he is plagued by the attentions of Eleanor Parker, who has nothing to offer him except wealth, breeding, wit and stunning beauty. Meanwhile his eldest daughter, Diesel, or is it Liesel, is petting heavily in the pergola with a singing postman. And here come the Nazis! How to escape? Improvising brilliantly, Julie and Christopher get married, enter the children in the Salzburg Festival, and walk to Switzerland under cover of the applause.

This is a partial use of an original idea by George Hurdalek, in which they were to walk to Stalingrad, surround the entire German army, and accept the surrender of General von Paulus.

31 December, 1978

Freezing fog situation

IT doesn't matter when the Beeb's weatherman, Mr Fish, wears a jacket that strobes like a painting by Bridget Riley. But it does matter when he warns us about something called a 'freezing fog situation'.

There is no such thing as a freezing fog situation. What Mr Fish means is a freezing fog. In the panic of the moment, when on television, I myself have employed the word 'situation' when it was not strictly necessary. Even now I find myself thinking of Mr Fish as Mr Fish situation. But Mr Fish situation has all day to rehearse his little bit of dialogue situation. There is no excuse for his situation getting into a saying 'situation' situation.

If the BBC, once the guardian of the English language, has now become its most implacable enemy, let us at least be grateful when the massacre is carried out with style. *Ski Sunday* (BBC2) was once again hosted by David Vine. The event was the downhill at Crans-Montana. In their new, filmy ski-suits, the contestants looked like Martian archaeologists who had arrived on earth, discovered a packet of condoms, and had tried them on over their entire body. Müller looked like beating Podborsky's time. Understandably excited, David once again chose words to convey something other than what he meant. 'And Müller is inside!' he bellowed. 'He is inside Podborsky by a long way!'

There was more of the same on *Superstars* (BBC1). This is the programme in which David Vine has Ron Pickering to assist him in the task of verbal evocation as sportsmen who are well known for being good at one thing strive to be a bit better than mediocre at other things.

The first show of the new series featured 'some of the most famous names and faces in twenty-five years of British sport.' Collectively, these were otherwise referred to as 'the great heroes of sporting legend of all time'. Respectively, they were called things like 'the Gentle Giant' and 'the Blond Bomber'.

Among the few great heroes of sporting legend of all time that I could actually recognise was Bobby Charlton, whose baldy hairstyle is hard to miss. For years now, as one chrome-dome to another, I have been trying to reach Bobby through this column in order to tell him that his cover-up can only work in conditions of complete immobility. If he took up Zen finger-wrestling there might be some chance of retaining his carefully deployed strands in place. But in a 100-yard dash against the Gentle Giant and the Blond Bomber the whole elaborate tonsorial concoction was simply bound to fall apart.

Bobby won the race, arriving at the finishing line with his hairstyle streaming behind his skull like the tail of an undernourished comet. Seemingly without pausing for breath, Bobby went straight into the mandatory victor's interview with David Vine. It was notable, however, that his coiffure had magically been restored to position – i.e., it was back on top of his head.

Fatuous chat matters less when the sport is worth watching. On *Grandstand* (BBC1) there were amazing scenes from Brighton, where China's number two table tennis player, Kuo-Yao Hua, narrowly defeated China's number four, Liang Ke-Liang. Mercifully the commentator's refrained from calling either of these men the Bandy-legged Barbarian or the Moon-faced Marauder. 'Ooh my goodness me, you really do run out of things to say!' yelled the stunned voice-over, running out of things to say.

For Kuo and Liang, the table merely marked the centre of the battlefield. They spent most of their time in the audience, returning each other's smashes. 'Ooh my goodness me, this chap could almost compete in hurdles as well as table-tennis!' screamed the voice-over brilliantly. This Chap was either Kuo or Liang: when they're so far away it's hard to tell them apart.

In fact the camera gave up the attempt to keep them both in shot. You saw This Chap in the distance returning a smash with a high lob that disappeared out of the top of the frame. There would then be a long pause, finally interrupted by the sound of another smash and the reappearance of the ball in low trajectory on its way back to This Chap. 'Who could argue that this is not first-class entertainment?' Nobody, so for God's sake shut up.

Grandstand also featured the Rose Bowl: University of Southern California v. Michigan. It becomes clearer all the time that American football leaves our kind looking tired. A voice-over at our end warned that we might find it 'a bit of a mystery to unfathom what's going on'. But really it was not all that hard to unfathom. Even when you couldn't follow the American commentators you could tell they were talking sense. The tactics and strategy were engrossing even when you only half-understood them. The spectacle, helped out by action replays of every incident from four different angles, was unbeatable.

Among the many startling aspects of the Rose Bowl was the fact that violence was confined to the field of play. Nor did any of the commentators find it necessary to remark that some of the players were white and others black – perhaps because the same applied to the commentators. This was a nice contrast with *Match of the Day* (BBC1), where an hysterical voice-over was to be heard commending 'the two coloured players' for 'combining beautifully'. The difference between commentating and Colemantating is that a commentator says things you would like to remember and a Colemantator says things you would like to forget.

21 January, 1979

Life on earth

A N intensive letter-answering operation situation mounted in response to an overwhelming readers' response situation to my remarks last week on the BBC's excessive use of the word 'situation' situation has left me in a state of prostration situation – i.e., knackered.

Only David Attenborough's miraculous new series *Life on Earth* (BBC2) has kept me sane. Two episodes have so far been screened. I have seen each of them twice. Slack-jawed with wonder and respect, I keep trying to imagine what it must be like nowadays to be young, inquisitive and faced with programmes as exciting as these. There can't be the smallest doubt that this series will recruit thousands of new students for the life-sciences. Where was David Attenborough when I was a lad? Being a lad too, I suppose. The difference between us is that he still is.

Fresh-faced and paunchless, Attenborough looks groovy

in a wet-suit. Female viewers moan low as he bubbles out of the Pacific with a sea urchin in each hand. Against all the contrary evidence provided by James Burke, Magnus Pyke and Patrick Moore, here is proof that someone can be passionate about science and still look and sound like an ordinary human being.

It is a lucky break that the presenter looks normal, because some of the life-forms he is presenting look as abnormal as the mind can stand. To Attenborough all that lives is beautiful: he possesses, to a high degree, the quality that Einstein called *Einfühlung* – the intellectual love for the objects of experience. Few who saw it will forget Attenborough's smile of ecstasy as he stood, some years ago, knee-deep in a conical mound of Borneo bat-poo. Miles underground, with cockroaches swarming all over him and millions of squeaking bats crapping on his head, he was as radiant as Her Majesty at the races.

Some of us are not as good as Attenborough at waxing enthusiastic when vouchsafed a close-up view of a giant clam farting. This happened many fathoms down on the Great Barrier Reef. As Attenborough zeroed in on the clam, it opened its shell a discreet millimetre and cut loose with a muffled social noise, visually detectable as a small cloud of pulverised algae.

Yet on the whole he compels assent. With the aid of film-footage so magnificent that it would have been inconceivable even a decade ago, he sets out to trace the history of life through 2,000 million years. The total effect is one of gorgeous variety. Even the single-cell life-forms reveal themselves to be bursting with ideas for getting about, eating, multiplying, etc. Further up the scale of complexity, the humblest sponge or Medusa is a whole universe of co-ordinated goings-on.

By the time you get to the invertebrates, you practically need a seat-belt, the aesthetic effect is so stunning. Here comes a flatworm rippling through the sea, like a rainbow-edged omelette in a hurry. Molluscs go laughing along in the other direction, like hysterical flying saucers. A transparent prawn looking as if Dürer had drawn it in liquid silver suddenly alters its position, as if he had drawn it twice.

Next week, the insects. I can hardly wait. But in the uproar of enthusiasm which will deservedly greet this series it should not be forgotten that the secret of its success lies just as much in the words as in the pictures. Attenborough has all the resources of technology at his disposal, but the chief attribute he brings to this titanic subject is his own gift for the simple statement that makes complexity intelligible. With him, television becomes the instrument of revelation. He makes me envious of my own children – members of a generation who will grow up with the whole world as their home.

Just as some life-forms are so perfectly adapted that they never need to change, so there are television formats that will be with us until Hell freezes over. Prominent among these is the thriller series set in or around the Mediterranean. The latest example is called *The Aphrodite Inheritance* (BBC1).

The venue this time is Cyprus. The hero, played by Peter McEnery, is out to avenge his murdered brother and recover the buried treasure. Or it could be that he is out to avenge his murdered treasure and recover the buried brother. The heroine is played by Alexandra Bastedo. Why is she canoodling on the beach with Stefan Gryff, who in these series usually plays the police chief, but on this occasion is appearing as Absolotl Preposteros, taciturn leader of the bad-shave heavies? Is she working under cover? She looks as if she is acting under water, but there is a good reason for that.

The good reason is the dialogue, which she and the hero are obliged to foist on each other in long, despairing interchanges. 'There's a lot of things I don't understand. Your part in this, for instance.' 'All we have to find out is who took the money and where it is now.' 'But who? And why?' 'It doesn't make sense.' 'Unless … ' 'Someone is using you.' 'The question is who? And why?' 'There must be someone here on Cyprus we can trust.'

But there is no one here on Cyprus they can trust, with the sole exception of the script-writer. They can trust him to keep on coming up with lines that mention Cyprus, so that nobody in the audience will fall prey to the delusion that the series is set in Dagenham.

In another part of the same plot, a man is on the run. One of the bad-shave heavies has shot him, which must be almost as painful as the bouzouki music yammering away on the sound-track. Consolation shows up in the form of Maria, the irrepressible young olive-plucker who is the proud owner of the only uplift bra here on Cyprus.

'Eet ees a good bed, eh?' Maria hisses irrepressibly, throwing him on eet. Apparently eet ees. But she, too, is after the treasure. Could she be working under cover? Bouzoukis plunk suggestively. Outside in the cobbled courtyard, the taxi-driver, Nikos Haknikaragos, has died of boredom.

Once in a Lifetime (Yorkshire) was all about Iain Brodie, who is raising wolves in order to pit himself against them in 'personal confrontation'. To show how well he gets on with wolves, Ian went into the cage with a she-wolf called Sylvia. 'Take it easy, Sylvia. *Take it easy!* AAGH! Ooh, Christ! Barry, I must have help!' It didn't augur too well for the forthcoming personal confrontation.

28 January, 1979

Exploring the medium

IT needed Lindsay Anderson, director of *The Old Crowd* (LWT), to bring out a quality in Alan Bennett's writing which had hitherto lain dormant – crass stupidity.

Previously Bennett had been the helpless, shackled prisoner of his wit, sensitivity and insight. Secretly he was crying out for someone to spring him loose, so that he could set about doing what the real, committed playwrights do – i.e., make large, vague and hectoring statements about Bourgeois Society, of which they know little, and the Human Condition, of which they know less. But no ordinary director could play Fidelio to Bennett's Florestan. It would take a special kind of genius.

Lindsay Anderson was that genius. We have it on the authority of a charmingly gullible article in the *Guardian* that the first task Anderson set himself was to go through Bennett's script and take out the jokes. The chief factor inhibiting a breakthrough into true seriousness was thus removed at a blow, leaving a nebulous story about some hazily defined types moving aimlessly about in a half-furnished house. With the script sounding like Bertolt Brecht's rewrite of *Hay Fever*, it only remained to give it a television production that would make it look like D. W. Griffith's version of *Duck Soup*.

If Anderson had brought nothing but his talent to the job, the show would have been all over in five minutes. Luckily he had something more formidable to contribute – the power of his intellect. Anderson is certain that Bourgeois Society is crumbling. His way of conveying this is to give you a close-up of a ceiling cracking. It would be a trite image if it were merely casual, but supported by the focused energy of the director's mind it attains a pinnacle of banality that can only be called heroic.

Actors love Anderson. They give him everything. Such force of personality is not to be despised. But actors are not necessarily the best judges of a director's quality. Like anybody else, only more so, they want to be needed. They tend to admire the kind of director who gropes for what he wants, since it gives them a chance to show him what they can do. Jill Bennett will probably go to her grave convinced that it was a great creative moment when, in rehearsal, they worked out the details of how she was to have her toe sucked. To the dispassionate viewer, however, the relevant sequence looked exactly what it was – a distant, giftless echo of Buñuel.

167

This was Anderson's first television production. Characteristically he was eager to Explore the Medium. There were shots of the cameras to show you that television plays are shot with cameras, etc. By such means a few television directors built short-lived reputations back in the 1950s. Nowadays the tyro director is expected to get over that sort of thing in training school. Like good directors in any other medium, the good TV directors – Gold, Gibson, Lindsay-Hogg, Moira Armstrong and all the rest – rarely draw attention to their technique. If they did, they would have a better chance of being noticed by the thicker critics, but their work would add up to less.

The whole enterprise has been very instructive, which is why I have used so much space on it. The chief lesson to be learned is that even a writer as intelligent as Alan Bennett can fall prey to the delusion that solemnity equals seriousness. Only a lurking desire for respectability could have led him to deliver his work into the hands of Lindsay Anderson. The result was inevitable.

'It really is extremely sophisticated for a television play,' announced Anderson, warning us with customary hauteur that we would probably not be able to cope with the intensity of his vision. Actually, compared with even an ordinary television play like *Cold Harbour*, *The Old Crowd* was so unsophisticated that it could scarcely be said to exist.

As far as the text goes, Bennett must be given the benefit of the doubt. When the jokes went, the play's point went with them, since with a writer like Bennett the jokes are not decoration but architecture. People like Lindsay Anderson can never learn what people like Alan Bennett should know in their bones: that common sense and a sense of humour are the same thing, moving at different speeds. A sense of humour is just common sense, dancing. Those who lack humour are without judgment and should be trusted with nothing.

Brian Gibson, a director of real accomplishment, was in charge of Denis Potter's new play *Blue Remembered Hills*

(BBC1), in which adult actors, led by Colin Welland, pretended to be children. This was a bold conceit on Potter's part. Gibson helped him get away with it. An outstandingly tactful handler of actors, Gibson has been known to coax professional performances out of ordinary people, so there is almost no limit to what he can get out of professionals. I had never thought the day would come when I would find Colin Welland sympathetic, but in huge short pants and a brutal haircut, blubbing and shouting and making aeroplane noises, he was like one of your own callow embarrassments come back to haunt you.

The dialogue was Potter at his best, but doubts remain about how good that is. As far as I can remember from my own childhood – which took place, admittedly, altogether elsewhere – little boys are very specific about things like the names of aeroplanes. But some of the talk rang too many bells to be ignored. The my-dad-can-beat-your-dad routines were groan-provokingly authentic.

Helped by Gibson's effortlessly fluent cameras, the dialogue echoed through a forest as big as the world. At the end of the play the merry band contrived to burn a retarded boy to death in a barn. Let's hope this was fantasy and not one of Potter's real reminiscences of childhood, otherwise the police might be getting in touch. 'Mr Potter? Just a routine inquiry, sir. Couldn't help noticing in your very fine play the other night ... '

4 February, 1979

No credit for Puccini

IN *World of Sport* (ITV) there was cliff-diving from Acapulco and women's surfing from Hawaii. The cliff-diversprayed that the tide would come in while they were on their way down. Two of the women surfers were called Jericho Poppler and Sally Prange.

Taking leave of its senses, BBC1 screened *Seven Seas to Calais*, which some people fancy for the title of the worst film ever made. Australia's own Rod Taylor plays Sir Francis Drake. 'Let's foller their tracks,' he says, in Elizabethan tones, holding his arms slightly out from his sides to indicate the bulk and power of his lateral muscles.

John Mortimer fronted *Shakespeare in Perspective* (BBC2), introducing *Measure for Measure*, shortly to follow on the same channel. Speaking from the Inns of Court and the law courts themselves, Mortimer eloquently expounded the play's 'two great conflicting claims', justice and compassion. He also spoke about two great conflicting claims in Shakespeare's mind, namely the impulse towards order and the distrust of authority. So finely judged was his whole address that the following play seemed like an illustration of it.

The play proper, directed by Desmond Davis, had the best costumes and decor of the Bardathon so far. *Richard II* looked a touch more convincing, but that was probably because they turned the lights out, so that your imagination could work in the dark. Here it was all sunlight, yet the effect did not run shallow. The perspectives were well planned and properly crowded. It could have been old Vienna. At worst, it was a TV studio making a pretty good stylised shot at appearing not utterly different from what Shakespeare might just conceivably have thought old Vienna looked like.

Tim Pigott-Smith spoke so well as Angelo that you felt a glittering career was assured, and that he might therefore care to think about simplifying his name, since 'Tim' will date and 'Pigott' somehow suggests horses. 'Timothy Smith' would be more appropriate to an actor with a long future. The ladies were excellent. Impersonating Maria, who for some reason resents being abandoned by the dreaded Angelo, Jacqueline Pearce was a picture, and Kate Nelligan gave Isabella her formidable all.

A great gift is always an accident, but Miss Nelligan can be complimented for the sheer intelligence with which she guards her talent. She is a keen student of her lines, using her voice first and foremost and relying on her beauty last and least. As Isabella she gave only one reading that sounded even slightly false. (In the half-line 'To use it like a giant,' the word 'use' should be stressed, or else the argument is lost.) In all other respects she was clear-headed moral outrage personified. The Duke did a lot of wise nodding, especially in the last scene, when Isabella, instead of kicking him in the crutch for mucking everybody about, seemed willing to marry him.

One Fine Day (LWT), the latest in the series of Six Plays by Alan Bennett, showed the author on good form. It was too long and it sometimes sounded thin, but it was a subtle text that was well served by the director, Stephen Frears.

As far as Alan Bennett is concerned, there is really no substitute for the way Stephen Frears directs, since Bennett has by now taken to employing such an economical style of writing that the merest clumsiness from the camera would shatter the whole effect. In *One Fine Day* Dave Allen, going legit, played a real-estate salesman called George who was having qualms about modern life, with particular reference to the architecture of office blocks. With Puccini coming in through his earphones, *Weltschmerz* was going out through his eyes.

There was a lot of Puccini. 'No Credit for Puccini' would have been a good title for the play. Puccini helped you guess at George's interior state. There was very little dialogue to help you to do that. Most of the good things were said by Robert Stephens, playing George's awful boss. George rebelled, left home, and camped in the office block he was supposed to sell. Finally he unloaded it on the Japanese. In a way that was not made quite clear, he had rediscovered himself.

About five years ago Bennett appeared on one of those afternoon shows Thames puts out for affluent housewives with a Hitachi in the kitchen. Bennett was inveighing against modern architecture. The interviewer asked him to give an

In the *Circus World Championships* (BBC1), escapologist Mario Manzini, awesomely clad in crash helmet, strait jacket, shackles and handcuffs, dangled upside down thirty feet above the sawdust ring from a burning rope. The rope burned too well and Mario came down early. 'That ... obviously not meant to happen ... now being helped from the ring.' But all bad vibes were dispelled by the trapeze competition between the Oslers and the Cavarettas, in which girls of incredible pulchritude turned triple somersaults. It was an air-show for lechers, a Freudian Farnborough of flying crumpet.

25 February, 1979

Kodswallop

CROMWELL left so horrible a legacy in Ireland it's no wonder the English should want the whole subject covered up. Perhaps only through fiction can they face the facts. This hypothesis was lent weight by *I'm a Dreamer, Montreal* (Thames), a sensitive and penetrating new play by Stewart Parker.

Bryan Murray, an engaging young actor, played Nelson, a Belfast boy who worked in a music library by day and sang with a semi-pro dance band by night. Filling his head with old songs and dreams of fame, Nelson tried to remain oblivious of his surroundings. But his surroundings wouldn't let him. A bomb destroyed the music library. One of the band's gigs turned out to be an IRA rally. The British Army hauled him in for questioning. The girl he had fallen for stood revealed as the mistress of a psychopath, who carved him up by way of discouragement.

Since the carving-up had been inflicted on his behind, Nelson had to stand up going home on the bus. It was late at night. He was the only passenger. The driver was singing 'I'm a Dreamer, Montreal'. Nelson told him the real words ('I'm a Dreamer, Aren't We All?') and the driver realised he had been singing it wrong all his life. It was too subtle to be symbolism, but there were grounds for thinking that Nelson had begun to work the difficult double trick of seeing things as they were and yet remaining unembittered.

The director, Brian Farnham, deserves high praise. Like Stephen Frears with *Cold Harbour*, he transmitted the feeling of urban fright with such a delicate touch that you never felt you were being got at by anything except reality. A special nod should go to the casting director Rebecca Howard, who peopled the screen with depressingly believable-looking hard cases. As the dream girl, Jeananne Crowley was just right.

Casting was one of the weak points of another interesting new play, Alma Cullen's *Degree of Uncertainty* (BBC1). But Jennie Linden was excellent in the central role of Josie, a 37-year old mature student struggling to get a degree from a Scottish university while bringing up three children. At certain times Josie was also struggling against some pretty stiff dialogue. Next time Alma Cullen might try to be less emphatic about making her points, which on this showing are strong enough not to need spelling out.

Josie was serious. Most of the younger students were not. Nor, alas, were some of the faculty, especially the soulful lecturer who, after he had grown tired of having an affair with her, shopped her to the examining committee for having an unoriginal mind. His was a character I would have liked to see further explored, since the ethical question involved is seldom touched upon.

Almost every university department I have ever heard of is haunted by at least one Lothario who sees nothing wrong with trying to screw the prettier students. The concept of academic freedom usually ensures that such conduct goes unpunished, even though it is patently unfair to the screwed and the unscrewed alike. Jennie Linden evinced the appropriate moral outrage.

The Serpent Son (BBC1) is a three-part series in which the Oresteia of Aeschylus is to be made available to the modern viewer in a translation by Frederic Raphael and Kenneth McLeish. Only one instalment has so far been screened, so it would be decent to reserve judgment. But it is legitimate to convey one's initial impressions. Among these is the impression that the heyday of the house of Atreus was an era rich in synthetic fabrics.

Denis Quilley played Agamemnon. Quilley has a classic face — i.e., finely chiselled and pugilistic at the same time. The two supreme classic faces of the twentieth century were conferred on Marlon Brando and the late Elvis Presley, but Quilley's will do at a pinch. Unfortunately it was hard to stop one's attention straying from his physiognomy to his apparel and coiffure. Dressed simultaneously as the Last of the Mohicans and the First of the Martians, he sported a Sam Browne belt, leather pedal-pushers, dreadlocks and a fringe. For the purpose of going away to the war and coming back afterwards, he was equipped with a suit of armour that strongly suggested American football. Perhaps the Trojan war had been transferred to the Rose Bowl.

Aegisthus also had a bulky carapace, which he seldom took off. It was studded with large nails, or small bollards. These made it very difficult for him to sit down. To prove this, the producer made him sit down as often as possible. The top girls looked no less remarkable. As Klytemnestra, Diana Rigg had a wardrobe of Pocahontas numbers for day wear. They came with a complete range of Inca, Aztec and Zulu accessories. But it was *en grande tenue* that she really knocked you out. The bodice of her evening gown featured a gold motif that circled each breast before climbing ceilingwards behind her shoulders like a huge menorah. It was a bra mitzvah.

Between the ruling class and the common people lay a

wide discrepancy of income. While the aristos had obviously been dressed by Jap, Courrèges and Zandra Rhodes, the lower orders were clad in rags. These were not, however, ordinary clothes that through long wear had ended up as rags. These rags had been *designed* as rags. Male members of the chorus wore shaggy jock-straps and hairy plimsolls under their rags. Women members wore their rags arranged as lap-laps. Refugees from Alternative Miss World or the Euro-vision Sarong Contest, they formed little heads-together backing groups while the men pounded out the rhythm with crooked staves. It was evident that there wasn't a straight stave to be had anywhere in Greece.

But it was Kassandra who took the biscuit. Helen Mirren played her as an amalgam of Régine, Kate Bush and Carmen Miranda. In a punk hairstyle the colour of raw carrots and frock left open all down one side so as to feature a flying panel of her own skin, she did a preparatory rhumba around the set before laying her prophecies on the populace. 'Now do you get it?' she hissed, but she was too late. Klytemnestra had persuaded Agamemnon to peel down to his gamma-fronts and take a bath. Blood mingled with the Pine Essence. Fancy things were done to frame the image. The whole deal looked like a dog's breakfast.

In the continuously intoxicating *Life on Earth* (BBC2) David Attenborough has reached the birds, by way of the reptiles. Among the principal reptilian attractions was a garter snakes' group grope. Gang-banging each other com-pulsively, they curled and writhed in their hundreds. New garter snakes were born entire and joined in. But the Bad Sight of the Month was a chameleon eating a cock-roach. It made a noise like a bottle of milk falling on a stone doorstep.

11 March, 1979

You gonna know!

L ATE getting back from America, for reasons which in due course I will explain at length, I spent only half the week watching television in Britain. The other half I spent watching television in Los Angeles, Chicago and New York.

As always, American television was a salutary reminder of what we are not missing. In the evening there are sometimes a few passable shows, but too much of what happens at night is like what happens during the day, and almost everything that happens during the day is like the end of the world. If only the quiz shows were the worst programmes on offer, American daytime television would be merely disgusting. There are, however, the evangelists, any of whom is enough to make you fall to your knees praying to see a quiz show instead.

In Chicago you get evangelists beamed at you from all directions. Jimmy Swaggart comes from across the Canadian border. 'Two prostitoots off the street and they *knew*! They *knew* when they got saved! You gonna *know* when you get saved you gonna *know* when you get saved gonna *know* you gonna *know* you gonna KNOW!'

But Jimmy is only warming up. Not only has he said all that without taking a breath, he has said all that without ceasing to smile. The time has come to turn serious. He closes his eyes. 'Oh God oh God oh God oh God oh *God*,' he intones. For a moment the viewer is worried about Jimmy's state of health. Is he having a heart attack? Has a hernia given way? Is he suffering from the delayed consequences of having zipped himself up at the wrong angle? 'Oh God oh God oh God oh God I pray that those who watch us over television, help them to *know* that JESUS is the only answer.'

Jimmy, like all the other television evangelists, looks like the host of a quiz show. The quiz show hosts all look like one another. Each looks as if a team of cosmetic dentists has capped not just his teeth but his whole head. On top of the resulting edifice flourishes a wad of hair transplanted from the rear end of a living buffalo. A quiz show host is as ageless as a Chinese politician. From the beginning of the show to the end, every day for ever, he says not a single spontaneous word. Even more disturbingly, the contestants don't either.

Intelligent Americans will tell you that the television quiz show is an art form. As one who likes pop culture, I am usually susceptible to such arguments, but there is a line to be drawn. It can be drawn at the point where a formula is too dead for variations on it to be interesting. Similiarly there is a limit to the sense in which it is true to say that people should be given what they want. The limit can be set at the point where the spectacle on offer ceases to be human. There is something inhuman about training quiz show contestants to jump up and down with excitement, faint with surprise and yell lines of special material even more fatuous than the stuff the host is reading off his cue cards.

Shows like *Card Sharks* and *The Price Is Right* can be regarded as typical. There are plenty more where they came from. After an introductory fanfare plugging Puppy Chow, Purina Cat Chow or Minute Made ('Mom, look at all those beautiful ornges!'), the host sways into position, buffeted by a gale of applause. They are applauding him for merely being alive – as well they might, considering what his head has been through on the operating table. The host introduces the first contestant, Rancine Zilchberger from Whang, Colorado. Rancine is blown sideways by a hurricane of applause. They are applauding her for being a resident of Whang.

When Rancine straightens up, she reveals the fact that she is a medical student. This time the applause assumes the proportions of a tornado, distorting her features with its pressure. Rancine is no oil-painting at the best of times, but there is no law which says that human beings should look beautiful. What they should look is human.

Rancine, however, has been encouraged to behave like a cheer-leader. Having chosen another card, or guessed another price, she hammers her desk top with her fists, chews he nails, rolls her eyes, and jumps up and down. When, amid an apocalypse of applause, it turns out that she has won, she screams and clutches her throat, strangling herself with ecstasy. Take a look at those hands. One day they could be operating on you.

Back in Britain, it is almost a relief to turn on *Blankety Blank* (BBC1), hosted by Terry Wogan. True, this is an American format, which has merely been transplanted like a tuft of hair. But compared with an American quiz show host, Terry Wogan is Doctor Johnson. He is capable of the occasional spontaneous remark. It is not a very memorable occasional spontaneous remark, but he is capable of it. On top of that, it is almost certain that most of his head is composed of the original tissue. Many times in the past I have made jokes about Terry's bionic appearance. It was wrong of me to do that. I see now that he is full of those redeeming flaws without which, as Degas insisted, there is no life.

Among the contestants is Nicholas Parsons. How wrong, how needlessly cruel, one has been about Nicholas Parsons. He is not, in fact, the chortling twit that he appears. By American standards he is an improviser of dazzling prowess. And Eddie Waring is there too — Eddie whose handling of the English language, it now becomes plain, is a triumph of sustained virtuosity. Together they all set about the task of filling in the blanks. Nobody in his right mind could give a blank about the results. The whole format is a load of blank. But at least the people concerned retain a spark of life. It is not much comfort, but it is something.

Gavin Millar fronted an interesting *Arena* (BBC2) about the Hong Kong film industry, whose executives tirelessly advanced the proposition that their uneducated audience needed simple fare. Scenes of bad actors kicking one another were shown – mere samples of films which consist entirely of the same bad actors kicking one another over and over again.

Omnibus (BBC1) defied precedent by screening a good programme. The subject was Natalia Makarova. Clement Crisp wrote and narrated with appropriate awe, but the decisive component was Derek Bailey's brilliant directing. Shooting and editing with unfaltering fluency and tact, he did for Makarova what he did for Lynn Seymour in the *South Bank Show* devoted to *Mayerling* – i.e., he brought out the discipline that underlines the magic, and thus made the magic seem more magical than ever.

1 April, 1979

That's right, yeah

ALMOST everyone in the Land of the Media got an award last week. *The Fifty-First Hollywood Academy Awards* (ITV) was a ceremony exactly answering its host Johnny Carson's description of it – i.e., 'two hours of sparkling entertainment spread over a four-hour show'.

Carson rose above the occasion like Gulliver in Lilliput. Alone among those present, he had a sense of humour and consequently a sense of proportion. Everybody else was swept away by the American inability to think small. So was the set. Not even Carson was immune from being attacked by the orchestra, whose various sections were seated in separate shells that moved around like dodgems. The nominated songs were what finally led me to tune out, unable to stand any more.

The British Rock and Pop Awards (BBC1) was an altogether less grand occasion. So inconsequential that it wasn't even offensive, it had the lasting importance of someone breaking wind in the middle of a hurricane. The *Nationwide* team claimed responsibility, along with Radio 1 and the *Daily Mirror*. Apparently the viewers, listeners and readers of these three media outlets had all scribbled in to vote for their favourite artists and albums. The venue was the Café Royal, once the haunt of Oscar Wilde and other *fin de siècle* wits, but now resounding to the shafts and sallies of Bob Wellings and Kid Jensen.

Bob is a *Nationwide* standby. Square as a brick. Kid is some sort of disc jockey. He has a face to match his name. Like many people in the pop world he has apparently not considered the likelihood that a time will come when the personality he has adopted will no longer be matched by his appearance, but for the moment there he is – a typical British DJ, right down to the American accent. Bob welcomed us to 'a moment for which we've all waited ... Britain's biggest ever national pop music popularity poll.'

It was a typical music business occasion. The speakers were tongue-tied and the audience was drunk. The stars made it clear that they were doing the event a huge favour by turning up at all. The representative of the Electric Light Orchestra, which won the Best Album award, was unique in having bothered to prepare a speech of acceptance. 'That's right, yeah. It's fantastic, this. We can't believe it. It's wonderful. Yeah.'

Bob and Kid hailed the Bee Gees as a British triumph. One of the Bee Gees lolled into view. Then Kid gave the game away. 'Is there any chance of a tour of Britain in the near future?' It transpired that the Bee Gees were in America most of the time. Still, one Bee Gee had turned up. Kate Bush had turned up too. Receiving her award, she congratulated herself for being in attendance. 'It was well worth it, reely.'

Everest Unmasked (HTV) started with a question. As the mountain loomed in vision, an awe-fraught voice-over asked: 'Is it possible to climb Everest and stand on its summit without using oxygen? *Even more important*, is it possible to return without brain damage?' The italics are mine. What he should have said, of course, was 'even *less* important'. No importance of any kind can nowadays be attached to the increasingly routine business of climbing Everest. Mad Japanese poets have gone up it on skis. The West Helsinki chapter of Mensa have been up it on pogo-sticks. The San Diego skateboard expedition is even now nearing the summit. Régine has plans to open a club up there. There is something to be said for man testing himself against the unknown. Where boredom sets in is when man tests himself against the known.

Star of the new expedition was a German called Reinhold Messner. Insulated against the cold by plastic boots, silk knickers, eiderdown-lined jump suit, three pairs of gloves, two hats and a beard. Reinhold positioned himself against the pitiless Himalayan skyline and explained why the challenge he was about to face was of crucial significance for the history of the human race. 'It is inneresting to try zis climb whizzout oxychen … what is important to explore is myself.' Reinhold forgot to add that exploring Reinhold's self was important mainly to Reinhold. For the rest of us, exploring Reinhold's self was bound to rank fairly low on any conceivable scale of priorities.

Up they strove o'er col and cwm. 'This is what separates the men from the boys,' warned the voice-over. Playing strange instruments, monks in lonely monasteries placated the gods. Hoo-woo. Bong. Sherpas loyally fell into crevasses. One of them was crushed to death 150 feet under an ice-fall. Another had to be brought down on a stretcher and sewn back together. Obviously the sheer volume of tourist traffic is tempting the previously sure-footed Sherpas to work hazard-ously long hours, despite the guide-lines laid down by their union, NUTCASE – the Nepalese Union of Trained Clim-bers Assisting Suicidal Expeditions.

Reinhold made it to the top. But the peril was not over. There was still the danger of brain damage – or, in Reinhold's case, further brain damage. The chances were that this would first manifest itself in the form of burst blood-vessels in the eyeball, loss of memory, impaired speech functions and the sudden, irrational urge to participate in stupid television programmes. Most of these symptoms duly appeared. Nevertheless Reinhold's achievement could not be gainsaid. He and his friends had proved that it is not enough to risk your neck. It is in the nature of man to risk his brains as well. Fighting his way upwards through drifts of empty beer cans and Kentucky Fried Chicken cartons, Reinhold had added his name to the select few thousand who have conquered the Lonely Mountain.

15 April, 1979

Busy old night

As Election Night dawned, if a night can dawn, only one question throbbed in the mind of the tension-fraught viewer. Was the BBC on its way out of power? Was it ITN's turn to rule? All right, two questions.

By 11 p.m. both campaigns are in full swing. The BBC team is full of comfortably familiar faces. Perhaps too familiar. Their leader, David Dimbleby, looks increasingly like his father. David Butler is still the psephologist. As of yore, Robin Day is all set to interview aggressively. Nobody pretends that Robert McKenzie and his Swingometer have not got whiskers on them. Angela Rippon, though she has not done this sort of thing before, looks as if she has been doing it all her life. Perfectly relaxed, she is backed up by a £200,000 computer called Rover, as if to prove that a woman plus a £200,000 computer is the equal of any man.

Leading the ITN team, Alastair Burnet is another veteran. Nor are Peter Snow and Leonard Parkin precisely unrecognisable. But Martyn Lewis is a refreshing new face and Anna

Ford, instead of being anchored to a £200,000 computer, is daringly out in the field like a female Rommel. Clearly ITN's budget is but a fraction of the BBC's. But there are more important things than money. Morale matters too.

For the BBC, Michael Charlton is 'with Mrs Thatcher'. It is quickly apparent that being with Mrs Thatcher means standing outside her house at No. 19 Flood Street, Chelsea. 'I can tell you that she's in the small upstairs sitting-room ... possibly watching the box.' David presses for more information. Michael penetrates the wall of the small upstairs sitting-room with his X-ray vision. 'There's no change in her condition ... she remains buoyant.'

For ITN, Anna Ford is also with Mrs Thatcher. Judging from the background' she must be standing about three feet away from Michael Charlton, but unlike him she is not equipped with X-ray vision. First blow to the BBC, whose studio is rife with informed speculation. David: 'It may be that we see a straight Tory victory ... but it is possible that ... there's even an outside chance of ... ' Bob and his Swingometer: 'I said she needs 4.5. According to the polls she's got 4.7.' Angela and Rover: 'Computer ... can draw pictures never seen on screen before.'

Neither side knows which constituency will declare first. Sorting white from grey ballot slips may take time. For the BBC, Frank Bough and his raspberry-fool tie are in position at Guildford. He raises the multiple ballot slip issue. 'One or two of the old biddies have had a little bit of trouble.' Back in the studio, Robin Day is smoking a large cigar. 'I shall be performing my usual humble function.' Still no action. For ITN, Alastair says, 'We'll be talking to anyone who's anyone,' as the camera zooms on an empty chair that will later contain Shirley Williams. 'It's going to be a busy old night.'

Back to Michael Charlton in front of Mrs Thatcher's house. 'We know that she's in here.' David: 'Have you had any sign during the day or the evening of how she thinks things are going?' 'No.' Michael's X-ray vision is obviously no longer operational, and he is replaced by Martin Young. At ITN, Shirley Williams has arrived. The BBC goes back to Martin Young in front of Mrs Thatcher's house and Anna Ford swims into shot. ITN goes back to Anna Ford in front of Mrs Thatcher's house and Martin Young swims into shot. Anna: 'I think the door is opening. Here she comes!' Anna asks the front of Mrs Thatcher's head a question. Martin Young asks the back of Mrs Thatcher's head a question. Neither gets an answer, but once again Anna has scored a point.

The first result. ITN goes live to Glasgow Central while the BBC is still dithering back in the studio. ITN is already processing the result before the BBC knows it has even happened. David is on screen with someone else's voice coming out of his mouth. Shambles. Finally Rover gets into action and produces some graphs, diagrams and statistics. They are not as good as ITN's graphs, diagrams and statistics. The ITN computer, called VT 30 Display System, is clearly superior at all points. This could be a massacre.

At Smith Square, Mrs Thatcher gets out of her car and for 0.4 seconds speaks to Anna, woman to woman. The BBC representative is somewhere in the crowd, strangling in his own flex. The second result: Cheltenham. ITN is first again, screening the action and processing the result while on the BBC Angie is rabbiting on about a power cut causing chaos in some other constituency. At long last the Beeb screens a still of Cheltenham town hall, accompanied by silence.

But the fight is not over yet. ITN suffers a bad setback in Cardiff, where its man is caught standing in front of a doorway through which Mr Callaghan does not emerge. Back to the ITN studio, where John Pardoe and Michael Heseltine present a sharp contrast in hairstyles. Pardoe is saying that the impact of personality in politics can be immense. It is possible that he could have his own personality in mind. With the Liberal vote collapsing, he has to cling to something. He could always cling on to Heseltine's hair. By now it is after midnight and ITN is predicting a 65-seat Tory majority.

On the BBC Bob McKenzie is more cautious. Outdistanced by technology, his Swingometer stubbornly warns that the final result might be less dramatic. Peregrine Worsthorne is equally tentative. 'We all try to be wise before the event, but I find it much easier to be wise after the event.' Perry is a strong plus for the Beeb. Bob stands before the Battleground. 'This is the board which I hope we'll be coming back to very often, because it does tell the story as well as it can be told. Except by you, David.' Could Bob and his creaking devices still have something on the ball?

ITN's Julian Haviland catches Jim on the move. 'Prime Minister, sorry to confront you like this.' 'No comment.' A triumph for ITN. The Beeb boobs badly over the Angus South result. Rover gives the Tories 2,000 instead of 20,000. ITN has been saying that Swingometers are out of date, but the BBC is learning all over again that it can't do without Bob. As Mrs Thatcher arrives in Finchley, the BBC has pictures, but they are pictures of Anna Ford, 'There's a lady from a television channel I won't mention,' says David, 'I don't know where our chap is.'

At 2.30 a.m. the BBC's Rover is predicting a 74-seat Tory majority. But the BBC's Bob McKenzie keeps insisting that only his steam-powered mechanisms hold the truth. At about 3.15 a.m. in Cardiff, Callaghan challenges Pat Arrowsmith to come up on the platform and repeat her abusive remarks. She comes up on the platform and repeats her abusive remarks. At 3.45 ITN is inside Tory headquarters. All night ITN has been first with the most. But for the BBC's Bob McKenzie it has been a personal triumph. As both channels go off the air, the personnel are hollow-eyed, Rover and VT 30 are shamefacedly revising their estimates downwards, and only the Swingometer is fully alert, its cardboard arrow still pointing now where it has been pointing all night – at the right answer.

6 May, 1979

Zorba the Hun

Now that the incoming Tory Government has made greed patriotic, there is no use pretending that we aren't going to have a much easier time of it. Except, of course, for those of us who are going to have a much harder time of it.

But in one thing we are all united. We are all doomed to cope with five years of Mrs Thatcher's liturgical tones. She started quoting St Francis within minutes of becoming elected, and scarcely an hour had gone by before she was sounding like the book of Revelations read out over a railway station public address system by a headmistress of a certain age wearing calico knickers. By dawn of the next day she was doing a fair imitation of the Sermon on the Mount. Perhaps she is just nerving herself up for the miracles she will have to perform with the loaves and fishes.

Somewhere in one of the better decorated of the lower regions, Noël Coward is stretched out on a chaise-longue. Surrounded by onyx clocks, tall drinks and signed photographs of Gertrude Lawrence, he is looking at a television set in a satinwood cabinet. *Design for Living* (BBC1) has barely begun. Suddenly there is a snapping sound. Coward has just bitten through the stem of his ebony cigarette holder. What the hell have they done to his play?

A desperately nervous piece about three desperately clever people in love, it is not much of a play, principally because it is desperately short of good lines. But given lashings of style it could still be brought off. Unfortunately in this production most of the style was confined to the costumes, decor and props. Pretty clothes were hung on Rula Lenska, who played Gilda. Elegant tail coats swerved over the taut rear ends of the two young actors who played Gilda's lovers. Art Deco *objets d'art* stood in serried ranks on the mantelpieces and coffee tables, as if to illustrate a long article by Bevis Hillier. On sound, Marlene Dietrich was follink in luff again.

But nobody in the show except Dandy Nichols, who was pretending to be the maid, had any idea of how to underplay a scene. They all shouted their heads off while offering one another cigarettes from cigarette tins which you could tell were the genuine contemporary article from how scratched and battered they were. The implication was that fashionable people in the 1930s went about offering one another cigarettes from scratched and battered cigarette tins, while bellowing lines like, 'Whom do you love best?'

All three principal players held their cigarettes from underneath, like Russian spies. I suppose that there are photographs of Noël Coward doing this which could be advanced in favour of the argument that in a Noël Coward play there is really no other way to hold a cigarette. There are also plenty of gramophone records which could be adduced as evidence that Noël Coward and Gertrude Lawrence over-enunciated at all times. But they were in a *theatre* – or if they were not in a theatre were in a recording studio staffed by engineers too shy to tell them that they were not in a theatre. On television in 1979 it is not necessary to yell. There is nothing to be gained by it except strained vocal cords.

Most theatre is tripe now, and most theatre was tripe then. Distance lends enchantment, but the likelihood is that in the original production of *Design for Living* Coward and the Lunts were unbelievable and arch with it. It can be taken for granted that the average standard of acting which we see on television today is far better than the average standard of acting which prevailed in the theatre before the war. It is therefore doubly annoying to see actors on television behaving as if they were mixed up in a piece of bad theatre.

At one point, when Miss Lenska and her two lovers were screaming at one another particularly loudly while lighting half a dozen cigarettes each, I switched over to the film

Man without a Star on BBC2 and found Kirk Douglas looking subtle by comparison. Since Kirk Douglas could not hum a lullaby to a sleeping child without popping his eyes, gritting his teeth and focusing his dimple, it will be appreciated that the people from whom I was experiencing him as a relief must have been a long way over the top.

Far be it from me to intrude on Philip French's territory, but there are occasions when the films shown on television are too important to be ignored. *Attila the Hun* (ITV) is an example. Some experts place it among the All-time Bottom Ten, along with *Zarak, Written on the Wind* and *The Swarm*. For admirers of Anthony Quinn, this is perhaps the key film in his oeuvre. In *Zorba the Greek* he is Zorba the Greek, in *Lust for Life* he is Zorba the Frog, but in *Attila the Hun* he is Zorba the Hun.

The Roman empire is in decline. Attila is a rough diamond but he is imbued with energy. 'Lissename allayou,' he tells the Huns. 'This is an arpatoonity to carnker Rome!' Sophia Loren, playing a decadent Roman aristo, goes for him. He is her bit of rough. More macho than Attila they don't come. Attired in top-knot, ear-rings, green tights, gold-studded jock-strap and après-ski boots, he is one stunning hunk of Hun. Sophia's decadence is chiefly signified by the kind of décolletage that leaves even an experienced rapist like Attila shifting his feet awkwardly. She is all chiffon and angel food. He is all studs, spikes and greased thongs. Mad about each other, they advance on Rome, while kissing. It is not easy, especially on horseback.

It looks like curtains for the cradle of civilisation. But with the city walls in sight, Attila and his ravening horde are met by several hundred extras robed in white. The air is filled with celestial music, odd to the Hunnish ear. 'Strange sound. Sort of chanting.' The Christians – for these are indeed they – kneel and bid Attila wreak what wreck he reckons appropriate. Attila draws his extremely butch-looking sword and flourishes it aloft. But the word that springs to his cruel lips

is: 'Back!' And back the Huns go to Huntingdon, or wher-
ever it is they live, while a cross of light appears in the sky and
Sophia elopes with Carlo Ponti.

13 May, 1979

While there's Hope

M ARCUS AURELIUS was not the first to suggest that there
is a decent time to make an exit from public life. Entertainers, unfortunately, have always been apt to stick around
long after the appropriate moment. Having grown used to
being loved for what they do, they end up imagining that
they are loved for themselves, and so feel impelled to carry on
out of a duty to their public. Thus egotism and altruism are
fatally compounded, giving off a gas which corrodes the
entertainer's reputation as fast as it goes to his head, while
the critical onlooker falls unconscious.

None of the above paragraph, of course, applies to *Bob
Hope at the London Palladium* (ATV). Apart from having a bit
less memory to be thankful for, he is just as good now as he
ever was. But there is no need to go overboard about how
good that is. Standing up and delivering one-liners that
somebody else has written takes more nerve, but less skill,
than might appear. Of all the comic forms it is the most
limited. The comedian who never gets beyond wisecracks is
bound to stunt his own growth.

That was how Hope appeared on this show: a stunted
giant. It is less easy to describe Richard Burton, who flew all
the way from Mexico in order to help Hope be less funny.
Working together with the practised ease of two Scottish
football supporters in a revolving door, they delivered the
kind of patter which only those with their brains eaten away
by fame can imagine they are getting away with. 'Don't

forget, Bob, London is still talking about all your triumphs too. I mean ... ' 'You know, Richard ... ' 'Seriously Bob ... ' The biggest joke of all was supposed to be when Burton quoted scraps of Shakespeare, thus emphasising that the man doing all this slumming was really an actor of unquestioned stature. The inevitable comparison was with John Barrymore in his cups.

Hope spent most of the evening introducing the supporting acts, thereby illustrating the principle that in the final stages of fame you no longer have to do very much of whatever it was that made you famous in the first place. Leslie Uggams, who is not quite that famous yet, actually did some singing and dancing. (It is notable that Diana Ross, a comparably beautiful and talented black entertainer, is more famous than Miss Uggams and therefore nowadays spends the best part of her act talking instead of singing.) Raquel Welch was also among Hope's guests. She is the exception to the rule I have just outlined. By now she is famous enough to do nothing. Instead, she gives us her all.

Raquel was involved in a lengthy comic routine which required that she should pretend to sing and dance very badly. This she accomplished with ease. The trouble started when she reappeared *in propria persona* and tried to convince us that she can sing and dance very well. Thousand of pounds' worth of feathers, each plume plucked from the fundament of a fleeing flamingo, could not disguise the fact that she sings like a duck. As for her beautiful body, she has taught it to move in time, but the whole strenuous effort has been a triumph of determination over an invisible pair of diving boots. Hope looked on proudly. He had got what he came for, whatever that is.

Envious of *The Word* (ITV), the Beeb has imported a blockbuster American serial of its own. Called *Centennial*, it is adapted from a novel by James A. Michener and is destined to run for months on BBC1. In the early stages a fur trapper came splashing out of the untamed wilds in order to pitch hairy woo at Raymond Burr's daughter, played by the marvellous Sally Kellerman. 'If you survive de Indians,' said the trapper, describing life in the unknown, 'dere are de animals.' Miss Kellerman did her best to look lovelorn. What a comic actress of her stature was doing in an epic bore like this was a conundrum best left ravelled.

Crime and Punishment (BBC2) is better value than *Centennial*, although it need not necessarily have been so. Television can add psychological depth to writing like Michener's. From writing like Dostoevsky's it can only take it away. On the page, Raskolnikov's face does not reveal much. On the screen it belongs to John Hurt and reveals everything. His performance is a brilliant job of exteriorising interior turmoil. He is as expressive as the decor, which evokes old St Petersburg in all its teeming squalor. But the dialogue, by the late Jack Pulman, is necessarily flat, simply because dialogue can do only so much.

Half of the *South Bank Show* (LWT) was devoted to the painter Allen Jones, whose tastes, you will recall, run to ladies with their toes crammed into high-heeled shoes. It transpired that in weighing down and screwing up his anonymous lovelies with shackles, manacles, chains and rubber knickers, Jones is merely exploring a 'new possibility for restating the figure'. These were the artist's own words. He had several hundred more just like them. He was passionately insistent that 'the lengths you have to go to in order to get a pure response ... are extreme.'

What a pure response might happen to be was not defined. Presumably it is an unequivocal willingness to be stunned by the paintings of Allen Jones. I admire his dedication but can give only an impure response. As the author of the only Pirelli calendar that nobody bothered to look at twice, Mr Jones should realise that his females are competing for attention, not against other images, but against real females, and that this is a fight they are bound (if you will forgive the pun) to lose.

3 June, 1979

Not the chief

Q UIS *custodiet custodes?* It is a good idea for writers to
monitor the broadcasters, who tend not only to abuse
the English language, but to encourage the notion
that it is all right for everybody else to abuse it too. But who
will monitor the monitors? Reviewing a play in the *Evening
Standard* on Thursday, Milton Shulman wound up in fine style.
'Gracefully played and beautifully directed by Peter Wood,
I was impressed rather than moved by these chatty, elusive,
insubstantial people.' Here, I think, Milty does himself a dis-
service. He is neither played by an actor, nor told what to do
by a director. The role of Milton Shulman is taken, incom-
parably, by Milty himself.

Meanwhile Leonid Brezhnev was making what must surely
be one of his last appearances. Still made up for a bit part in
Planet of the Apes, Brezhnev was to be seen shambling around
Vienna, whither he had come to make his mark on the SALT
agreement. The cameras could tell you little about him.
Either he was barely alive or else he was already dead and
being operated by remote control from the Kremlin.

According to his official biography, which it took the whole
of the Central Committee's Marxist-Leninist Institute to
write, Brezhnev spent the late 1930s doing 'party work' in
the Ukraine. He was, in other words, engaged in the task of
killing people by the thousands. But in that ugly mug of his
there is no trace of any experience more haunting than acute
boredom.

The human face can tell you quite a lot about transient
emotions, a little about character, and almost nothing about
what the person wearing it has been doing with his life. I
would be surprised if anyone could have told what Gustav
Franz Wagner had been up to from just looking at his rather
distinguished features. Interviewed on *Panorama* (BBC1), he

193

gave the impression, to look at him, of being a man of some intelligence who had unfortunately been overtaken by senility. He is, however, or at any rate was, the man who did his best to make Sobibor extermination camp even more hellish than it was supposed to be.

Luckily we had more to go on than the way he looked. There was the way he sounded. It instantly became apparent that Wagner had the intellectual complexity of a turnip. 'I was not the chief,' he mumbled. 'I was the sub-chief.' Lest we had missed the point, he went on to explain that the chain of command stretched all the way up to the Führer himself. By the time the orders got down as far as Wagner there was no possibility of argument. 'I didn't have much responsibility.'

Wagner denied that he had ever looted the belongings of those who had been killed. 'It's against my deepest convictions.' Leaving aside the fact that the SS trafficked in loot as a matter of official policy, here was an instructive example of the universal truth that nobody believes himself to be without ethics. Clearly Wagner still credits himself with a highly developed sense of duty. Yet he made sure that the inhabitants of his camp died a thousand deaths instead of just one.

He made the other officers seem kind by comparison, so that one survivor still remembers them fondly as being, not sadists like Wagner, but reasonable men who imposed no unnecessary suffering as they got on with the job of gassing people on an industrial basis.

All the evidence suggests that Wagner enjoyed murdering people. He thus presents a less taxing moral problem than those of his colleagues who didn't particularly enjoy it, but went ahead and did it anyway. When he calls himself 'an ordinary man like anybody else' he mis-states the case. Nevertheless he is worrying enough. At the moment it looks as if the impact in Germany of the American TV series *Holocaust* will ensure that a statute of limitations on Nazi atrocities will not be imposed. There is, then, still a slim but heartening possibility that men like Wagner will be called to account.

Just because revenge is pointless — how can one man's eye pay for the eyes of thousands? — does not mean that there should be no reckoning, if only to clear the air of the euphemisms that insult the dead. 'We were engaged in top secret Reich work,' drones Wagner. Like Brezhnev's 'party work' in the Ukraine, this was the work of Satan and should be revealed for what it is to the generations who will have the dubious privilege of succeeding us.

Continuing its useful series of repeats, *Yesterday's Witness* (BBC2) once gain brought us Gergana Taneva, a quietly eloquent lady who survived Ravensbrück, perhaps for the specific purpose of giving us at least some idea of what life is like when people whose highest morality is to obey orders are controlling your fate. 'They were absolutely normal people,' she insisted.

She never even had the comfort of being able to blame her sufferings on a madman like Gustav Franz Wagner. The people doing these things to her were people like her. 'We learned not to be vocal about things.' Not to be vocal, that is, while your daughter or your mother, who had been worked to exhaustion before you had, was taken away in front of your eyes to be put to death.

In Nazi Germany there was no such thing as a miscarriage of justice, because there was no justice. The same has applied to the Soviet Union since the day of its inception. In a democracy like ours the law might be an ass but at least it exists. Not that to love the law necessarily means to love lawyers. On the whole one's dealings with the legal profession are best confined to regular watching of *Rumpole of the Bailey* (ATV). In Rumpole, it is by now clear, John Mortimer has created one of the truly durable television figures. Leo McKern has only to put that frazzled wiglet on his head and your evening is a success.

In the latest episode of his adventures, Rumpole defended a home-grown racist fanatic and got him acquitted. The message was that freedom of speech is a right which means nothing if it is not extended to those who abuse it. The judge was a racist himself. Luckily the law was not. As usual, Featherstone and Erskine Browne provided the necessary contrast to Rumpole's rumpole appearance. Already he is an adjective. He is also an idea.

'Malaysia has now said it won't be shooting boat people after all.' Thus ran the encouraging message on the news programmes. It was reported that the responsible Malaysian Minister, who had previously been quoted as announcing the intention of 'shooting them on sight', was now saying that he had only recommended 'shooing them on sight'.

Nobody in the boats was heard to laugh at this joke. In Thucydides, after the climactic battle, the winners put the losers in a hole without food or water, and wait. The only difference between then and now is that we can see it on television.

24 June, 1979

Carpenter the Rain King

O N both BBC channels, Wimbledon was back and Dan Maskell was back with it. 'Ooh I say! There's a *dream* volleh!' Too late now, alas, for Dan to become a popular singer. He could have had a big hit with 'Golleh golleh golleh Miss Molleh.'

But we should be grateful that Dan was born to be a tennis commentator. Wimbledon would be smaller without him. Even Harry Carpenter, who calls Wimbledon Wmbldn, is a necessary part of the scene, especially when he delivers his famous Rain Commentary. 'We're in for a feast of tennis over the next fortnight,' said Harry on the first day. 'It's going to be a wonderful Wmbldn.' Dan agreed. 'The Centre Court is absolutely bathed in the most lovely sunshine.' It was absolutely clear that both boys were on top form. 'There is the Duke, the President of the Club,' said Dan. 'And so ... a Royal occasion.'

Borg and Gorman shaped up to each other. After twenty-seven minutes of play the rains came. 'This is quite a sight in itself, the court cover being pulled across. It weighs a couple of tons ... they usually get a round of applause for this — there we are ... just having to ... sort it out ... the rain all the time falling on the surface ... perhaps as the rain is falling on that cover, it's time to remember how well Borg was playing.'

But most of that came from Dan. Measured against the standards of Rain Commentary set by Harry it was tame stuff. Harry himself came on screen to show how it should be done. 'And people quite happy to stand out there under their umbrellas and watch the covers being put on.' What makes Harry's Rain Commentary such a revolution in communications is the underlying assumption that the rain is fascinating in itself. Not quite as fascinating, perhaps, as Borg and Gorman hitting tennis balls at each other, but still pretty gripping.

Down it comes, bouncing on the covers, gradually accumulating in hundreds of differently shaped puddles. But notice the way some of the puddles are joining up! There's a positive lake forming near the base line! Yes, Wmbldn fortnight will always be the climax of the year for anyone interested in rain.

In the case of British Hope John Lloyd, Dan's inextinguishable patriotism found a worthy object. It will be recalled that John, after marrying the American champion Chris Evert, celebrated his good fortune by losing nineteen matches in a row. His opening singles match in these championships made it an even twenty. But in the first round of the doubles his luck turned. This was almost certainly due to psychic support from Dan. 'Ooh, bad *luck*, John!' cried Dan as John dinked a sitter into the net or beaned the umpire with his second service. Dan's waves of sympathy paid off. John, partnered by his younger brother Tony, took courage and won. Only the brave deserve the beautiful.

Meanwhile Jimmy Connors had unleashed his new tactic, the Early Grunt. Yes, Jimbo is grunting earlier this year. Tennis buffs will be aware that after his marriage to the afore-mentioned Christ Evert failed to take place, the bullet-headed ball-bouncer consoled himself by cleaving unto Patti McGuire, *Playboy's* all-time most gorgeous gate-fold. Wedlock has brought wisdom. Once, in moments of crisis, he would take out and read the famous Letter from his Mother – always a heartening event for his opponent. Now he has taken to grunting loudly at the instant of hitting the ball instead of just afterwards. Confused opponents try to hit the grunt instead of the ball.

As the first week of Wmbldn drew to a close, three-time winner Bjorn Borg suffered a groin strain, or grorn strajn as it is known in his country. The possibility that he might be eliminated through injury was greeted with universal, and well-justified, alarm. Simply by doing nothing repulsive, Borg has established himself as the most attractive young champion in sport today.

But more of Wimbledon next week. For the present it behoves me to assess *The Mallens* (Granada), billed as 'a story of scandal, passion and romance' in seven parts, of which three have been transmitted so far. People have written in to ask if I am as enthralled as they are. The answer is that I am even more enthralled than they are. Time between episodes is time wasted. Seldom has the neurotic turmoil of nineteenth-century scandal, passion and romance been so transfixingly rendered. Beside *The Mallens*, *Wuthering Heights* reads like the letters of Madame de Sévigné.

The central scandal, passion and romance is the liaison between Squire Thomas Mallen (John Hallam) and gover-ness Anna Brigmore (Caroline Blakiston). It is madness, their scandal, passion and romance. Yet mere reason is powerless to curb the force of emotion unleashed in both of them by the very sight of each other. 'Why does it always have to be like a rape?' 'That's what you love the best.' END OF PART ONE.

But these, like all great lovers, are more antagonistic than affectionate. 'We can't afford it.' 'Damn your afford it! Am I the master here or you?' Or have I got Squire Mallen mixed up with evil Donald Radlet? Both men share the same tempestuous hairstyle, although one of them has a white streak in it, like Diaghilev. 'When I think of the amount I must have drunk.' 'And the women.'

Behind locked doors, in shuttered rooms, innocent young girls lie sleeping in their shifts. But there are strange cries from down the corridor. Are they the cries of an animal in pain? No, they are the cries of Miss Brigmore as she lies in the Squire's powerful arms. As innocent young feet creep close, we see that the Squire and Miss Brigmore are once again lost in the tumultuous throes of. ... END OF PART TWO.

'You will not be happy if you marry Donald Radlet!' Here comes the great Northumberland horse down the muddy Northumberland lane. Flurp, flurp, flurp. 'Am I to go on living?' No less impressive than the evocation of scandal, passion and romance is the painstaking concern with period detail. 'A bottle of brandy costs *five shillings*.' Nothing brings back the past like a seemingly casual reminder about the changing value of money. ('A solid gold watch! Why, it must have cost at least *fourpence*.') But once again Squire Mallen and Miss Brigmore have collided on the stairs. Within seconds they are raining hot dialogue on each other. A foot-race to the nearest bedroom ends in a dead heat. END OF PART THREE.

1 July, 1979

Immaculate length of Borg

THE second week of *Wimbledon* (BBC1 and 2), known to Harry Carpenter as Wmbldn, had most of its climaxes early, if you will excuse the phrase.

'Well, there's a little sensation for you out there,' gritted Harry, as the brave but dejected McEnroe headed 'back to the loneliness of the locker-room'. There was another little sensation for us in Virginia Wade's defeat at the hands of Evonne Cawley. Virginia was the Last British Hope. In recent years she has learned to think in terms of representing herself rather than Britain, with the result that she has done better for Britain, but this year marked a return to her old status as the Girl on whom British Hopes are Pinned. Nobody in the commentary box – not even Ann Jones, who has been through the same ordeal herself – seemed to realise that having British Hopes pinned on you slows you down.

The crowd sighed resignedly. 'All the years', Ann intoned, 'they've had to struggle through with Virginia's hopes and fears.' Dan Maskell had the statistics ready. 'Eighteen years of it, Ann.' As Virginia swiped and hacked, a certain weariness crept into Dan's normally ebullient cries of 'Ooh I say!' Dan was disappointed. 'I have a feeling Virginia Wade hasn't been practising her lobbing.' Nobody contemplated the alternative possibility, which is that Evonne Cawley is the supreme technician in women's tennis and wins when she feels like it. What confuses the issue is that she hardly ever feels like it.

The match between Dupre of America and Panatta of Italy was the thriller of the tournament. Panatta is an extremely good-looking man if you like your ice-cream runny. Dupre, on the other hand, is no oil-painting. But the two men would have been evenly matched if Panatta had not been given a whopping initial advantage by the presence in the stands of a sizeable part of the population of Italy. From every Italian eating establishment in London the cooks and waiters had converged on Wmbldn in order to help their boy by hindering his opponent.

Dupre found his every error being cheered to the echo. Imprecations were hurled at him as he stood poised to smash. They did everything but sling spaghetti. The umpire was terrifically British about it all. Sitting with a stiff upper lip in his stiff upper chair, he seemed to be working on the principle that if you go on ignoring people long enough they will behave like gentlemen. This was a big mistake. The Italian contingent spend most of their lives under the pavements of Soho breathing steam. This was their day of glory and they had no intention of letting a little thing like fair play cramp their style.

In the commentary box there was wit to match the tension. 'Dupre ... having to contend, as you can hear, with not only the accuracy of Panatta's racket, but also with the racket in the stands.' After, but not before, Panatta's claque had helped him win the third set, the umpire finally gave voice. 'Will you please be quiet when the rallies are on?' The right idea, but the wrong language. The uproar continued unabated. Finally it started putting Panatta off, too, a fact that Dan was quick to spot. 'Yes, disturbing their own man, now, the Italians, I think.' Yes, but not as much as they had previously been disturbing his opponent. In the end the better man won, and Panatta headed back to the loneliness of the locker-room.

According to the smart money, McEnroe's exit meant that Thursday's men's semi-final between Borg and Connors would be, in effect, the final. Alas, it was a dud match. Connors has run out of answers to what Dan calls 'the immaculate length of Borg'. Connors likes the ball to come at him in a straight line so that he can hit it back in another straight line. When it comes at him in a curve he uses up half his energy straightening it out again. Borg hits nothing but curves. Connors was left with little in the armoury except his new weapon, the Early Grunt.

As I revealed exclusively last week, Connors now grunts at the same time as he serves, instead of just afterwards. Since the grunt travels at the speed of sound, it arrives in the opponent's court marginally before the ball does. Ordinary opponents try to hit the grunt. Borg was not fooled. Indeed he quickly developed a Swedish counter-grunt. 'Hworf!' grunted Connors. 'Hwörjf!' grunted Borg. 'Game to Connors. Borg, rather,' cried the umpire helpfully. There they were, the two best: Connors with the long feet and the shoulders growing out of his ears, Borg looking like a hunch-backed, jut-bottomed version of Lizabeth Scott impersonating a bearded Apache princess. Back went Jimbo to the loneliness of the locker-room.

If Wmbldn was too much for your blood pressure there was always the punishing boredom of *International Athletics* (BBC1), piped to your living room from Malmö, Sweden. Obviously Borg has more reasons than tax avoidance for living in Monte Carlo. If Malmö is a typical Swedish metropolis, then it's a wonder the country has produced competitors in any events other than the 1,500 metres sleep-walk and the triple yawn. Could Britain qualify for the Europa Cup Final later in the year? To do so they would have to beat the Bulgarians.

Pattering around in front of the empty stands came a pack of runners, temporarily led by our man Coates. 'And Coates testing out the field,' said David Coleman. From that moment you knew Coates was doomed. 'The British team might have hoped that Coates might have put one or two more between himself and the Bulgarian.' Translated into English, this meant that Coates, on whom British Hopes had been Pinned, was on his way back to the loneliness of the locker-room. Nevertheless Britain qualified for the final.

The *French Grand Prix* (BBC2) featured a nail-biting tussle for second place between Villeneuve (Ferrari) and Arnoux (twin-turbo Renault). The French television service knows how to shoot a Grand Prix. (The Spanish just point all their cameras at the leading car and forget the rest.) Good direction makes a lot of difference. If the cameras are parked at the end of the straight and confined to shooting with long lenses then the action slows to a crawl. If the cameras are off to one side, or up in the air, and pan with the cars as they go by, then you get some idea of why men should want to risk their lives at such a sport. It is simply a thrilling thing to do.

Fighting bulls is probably quite thrilling, but the moral picture is complicated by the fact that the bulls suffer. One of the several good things about the first episode of *The Wooldridge View* (BBC2) was that the bulls stood a better chance than the men of getting home alive. The event was the bull-run in Pamplona, where Wooldridge goes every year to test his courage and his capacity for wine.

Apart from anything else, the programme gave you some useful hints about how to run before the bulls. Clearly the best technique is to book your flight for the week after the event takes place, or else just not turn up at all.

8 July, 1979

Baebius lives!

SKYLAB fell on my defenceless homeland. On *News at Ten* (ITN), Reginald Bosanquet, overcome with disbelief, read his autocue one line at a time. 'Skylab broke up, with debris. Streaking across the night sky and heading. Thousands of miles across the ocean for Australia.'

At least Reggie wasn't entirely speechless. I'm bound to confess that I was, since until that point I had been an admirer of President Carter. But when they start strafing your own country with tons of red-hot supersonic junk you can't help wondering whether there might not be some substance in all those theories about US imperialism.

The advantage of being in possession of an all-embracing

political theory is that you need never be at a loss either to explain events or to propose their remedy. Marxists, for example, not only know exactly what is going on in Northern Ireland, they know exactly what needs to be done next. The more evident it becomes that Britain would be glad to get out, the more they are convinced that Britain is contriving to stay in.

The same line of thought can be found in Livy, Book XXII, where Q. Baebius Herennius, tribune of the people, is to be heard announcing that it was the war-mongering Roman nobles who first drew Hannibal into Italy, and that those who have it in their power to end the war are continuing it by trickery so as to serve their own ends.

While Q. Baebius Herennius was saying all this, what was left of the Roman army was doing its damnedest to wear Hannibal down. Eventually, by the patience and sagacity of Fabius, Rome was saved. I don't say that the same tactics will be of much use in Ireland. Indeed I have no idea what should be done in Ireland. All I am sure of is that Q. Baebius Herennius will always be with us. Herennius perennius.

My own all-embracing political theory, for what it is worth, is that an inordinate proportion of the world's misery is brought into being by all-embracing political theories. These might tend either to the Right or to the Left, but what they have in common is the unwavering conviction that ends justify means. In this respect, any attempt to choose between the two sides is pointless. Nor should anyone who finds himself in the middle feel weak on that account. Powerless yes, but weak no. If history is with anybody, it is with those who are not sure where it is heading.

The above profound reflections are advanced in lieu of an appropriate reaction to *Outcasts on the China Sea* (BBC2), the best programme I have yet seen on the dread-provoking subject of the boat people. As Q. Baebius Herennius knows, the boat people mainly consist of North Vietnam's historically outmoded middle class. The expropriators have been expropriated. Upwards of 45,000 of the expropriated expropriators have ended up on the island of Palau Bidong, a small lump of granite with no toilets. Here, while doing their ingenious best to keep their children's drinking water free of excrement, they wait to see what the world has in store for them next.

As Harold Williamson, the programme's tactful front-man, was careful to make plain, these are the lucky few. Most of the boat people died on the way. The price for risking almost certain death is a large fee payable to the Vietnamese Government, which according to judicious estimates has so far amassed about £700,000,000 out of this sad traffic.

One of the things they might care to do with the money is hire a good PR firm, since by now everybody except Q. Baebius Herennius and Jane Fonda must be starting to wonder whether Ho's benevolence, always supposing it existed in the first place, has been passed on to those who have succeeded him in the task of guiding the Vietnamese people towards their destiny.

What no Marxist can begin to contemplate is that Marxism might be the reason why Marxist States turn bloody one after the other. *Panorama* (BBC1) had a report on Czechoslovakia, where it appears that the signatories of Charter 77 are currently getting it in the neck. The programme's front-man, who shall be nameless until such time as he gets his wires uncrossed, tried to tell us that the reason why sound and picture were out of synchronisation throughout the item was that the film had been shot in secret. This was, of course, tosh. Some of the film had indeed been shot behind the unyielding back of the local secret police, but the reason why the whole lot was screened out of sync was a cock-up at the BBC.

As was only to be expected, the growing tendency of BBC executives to follow up the wrong decision with a prevaricating explanation has by now infected the screen itself. The Beeb is running short of human faces. But a broadcasting organisation mincing its words in order to ward off criticism is not the same thing as a whole State dreaming up a pack of lies and calling it a constitution.

In Czechoslovakia at the moment, the secret police are keeping the playwright Vaclav Havel on his toes by blocking up his drains and not allowing anyone to clear them. When President Nixon was caught pulling that kind of stunt he was very properly thrown out of office. But in the Marxist countries such practices are not against the law. They are the law.

In *State of the Nation* (Granada), Jeremy Isaacs was the peripatetic moderator of a discussion on how, when and whether to tell the truth about an imaginary country called Freedonia. In the grip of a repressive regime, Freedonia nevertheless runs a reasonably benign salt-mine. Is a story about a non-violent salt-mine still a story?

The assembled communications experts pretended to worry at this topic, although really there was little in it. The real question was about who should be sent on such a story, the reporter with an axe to grind or the objective reporter. Even here the point was missed. Nobody except Q. Baebius Herennius doubts that there is indeed such a thing as objectivity. Unfortunately, however, it is often only the reporter with an axe to grind who can summon up the energy to get in there and ask the awkward questions.

Fronting an excellent *TV Eye* (Thames) on the subject of Islam, the redoubtable Vanya Kewley once again demonstrated that it is possible to be passionate in the cause of decency. Her *Everyman* programmes for the BBC were copybook examples of how right-wing nightmare nations like the Philippines and Paraguay can be discredited without any implication that left-wing nightmare nations are somehow not so bad after all.

Kewley elegantly embodies the principle that the truth is absolute, even if our grasp of it is relative. Q. Baebius Herennius believes that the truth is relative and his grasp of it absolute. She can understand him, but he will never be able to understand her.

1 July, 1979

I'm a star!

MOST of the last five weeks I have spent in a Swiss clinic having my mind operated on to remove a recurrent audio-visual image of Magnus Pyke getting out of a strait-jacket. The condition, brought on by watching too much bad television, was aggravated by the last programme I saw before clocking off. ITV had already packed it in by that stage, so the Beeb must have been the culprit.

The programme was all about Brecht. It had been assembled by David Caute, who apparently finds something continuously invigorating about Brecht's gift for mis-stating the obvious. At the very moment when a self-satisfied-looking actor, dressed up as Brecht, laid his finger alongside his nose and said something tremendously knowing about Hitler, I heard a snapping noise inside my head. A cortical partition had collapsed.

After a month of surgery, recuperation and analysis, the nightmare is back under control. Capering images of Patrick Moore playing table tennis have retreated. I am ready to continue, and even prepared to admit that apart from the news from Ireland it has not been a particularly depressing week. True, ITV is still confining its transmissions to a soothing white-on-blue caption, but Auntie has begun to stir.

Should American courts allow television coverage of trials? Should the BBC show you the results if American courts allow television coverage of trials? Everybody concerned having agonised for the appropriate period and said Yes, we were in a position to wolf down three unswitchoffable episodes of *Circuit Eleven Miami* (BBC2). Screened on successive nights, this alternately – and indeed often simultaneously – gripping and repulsive trilogy recorded the trial, conviction and sentence of one Thomas Perri, a citizen of Miami who had allegedly killed an 86-year-old man in peculiarly disgusting circumstances.

'Hey, here I am!' cried Tommy as the arresting officers bundled him towards the camera. 'I'm a star!' Pop-eyed, rat-nosed and barely articulate, Tommy was hard to love. But part of what seems to me the overwhelming argument against cameras in courts is that people should not be found guilty and sentenced to death merely because you don't like the way they look.

The mainstay of the case against Tommy was a charmer called Stephen Weiss, who insisted that he had been Tommy's accomplice in the murder. Stephen looked and talked like an associate professor of linguistics at a small but high-powered university. The way Stephen told it, helping bring Tommy to justice was his plain duty to society.

'He was bringing *me* down,' Stephen complained. 'Somebody has to *eliminate* Tommy. He's *sick*.' Tommy, it transpired, was so sick that he could make an otherwise reasonable man like Stephen do almost anything. Tommy had told Stephen to stab the old man, so Stephen had stabbed the old man. 'Tommy told me to stab him. I *believed* in Tommy. I believed in him as a better criminal than I was.'

For saying all this, Stephen had been rewarded before the trial started with a guaranteed maximum sentence of fifteen years, which would apparently work out, with time off for good behaviour and television appearances, at a total time behind bars of about ten minutes.

By sheer force of personality Tommy had induced Stephen to co-operate in the task of beating and stabbing the old man to the point of death. But it was Tommy alone, according to Stephen, who had climaxed this process by kicking a ballpoint pen through the old man's head. We were shown photographs of what the old man looked like after this had been done to him.

It was hard to see why the perpetrator of such a deed should be kept alive at public expense. But equally there was no gainsaying the fact that apart from a set of fingerprints and a hank of hair, both of which Tommy might conceivably have left behind on an earlier visit, there was nothing to connect Tommy with the crime except Stephen's testimony.

The Mini (BBC1) was all about a British engineering feat which I had always been under the impression was a huge success, but it turns out that this doughty little car has actually been something of a flop. The five million sold should have been 25 million, but (a) the workers failed to make enough of them, and (b) the managers forgot to include a profit margin in the price.

2 September, 1979

Plonking

IT was during *The Italian Grand Prix* (BBC2) that the moment of revelation came. 'James Hunt, *comment!*' screamed Murray Walker. Whereupon James Hunt commented, pertinently and in a normal voice, thereby proving once and for all that for a television performer it is not absolutely necessary to talk like a freak – merely advisable to.

On *Tomorrow's World* (BBC1) the intelligent and extremely presentable presenter Judith Hann was notorious, until recently, for her ability to hold out against concerted pressure to talk like a freak. She had no trace of the plonking manner. Her eyebrows and lips moved normally, while her voice issued forth in a temperate range of tones, with all the stresses in the proper places. The other night I tuned in and found her bobbing and weaving like a prize fighter, each eyebrow striving to upstage the other every time she stressed a word, which happened, *at a reasonable* estimate, twenty *times* per *sentence*.

She still looked and sounded pretty good, but the plonking manner was already well developed, and unless she takes steps to purge herself of these habits she might find herself being asked to join *Nationwide* (BBC1). Ever the true home of the plonking manner, *Nationwide* will not hire a presenter unless he, or she, has a solid track-record of talking like a freak. Mere unnaturalness of emphasis is not enough. You have to frown when you ask yourself a question, look relieved when you supply the answer, half-laugh when the subject is light, half-sigh when it is grave.

Sue Lawley incarnates the plonking manner to such a degree that she can even laugh at Max Boyce, which nobody else except a million crazed Welshmen has ever been able to do. On Thursday evening's *Nationwide* Max plugged his new book – apparently some kind of anthology enshrining the squibs and puns with which he makes his benighted country-men laugh. Introducing Max to her public, Sue fought to contain her merriment, but it ke-hept bu-hubbling up.

The plonking manner does for presenters what make-up does for actors: it is something to hide behind. For many actors, make-up is a shield warding off the world. They can't relax until they've put it on. For all presenters, except the ones who are so freaky they talk like that anyway, the plonking manner is a way of preserving the self while letting the not-self make a fool of itself. It is a trick for survival which all but the most intelligent presenters acquire automatically.

To be one of those voice-overs which announce forth-coming programmes, however, needs special training. Only after the most complete brainwash is the new recruit ready to announce, as a BBC1 voice-over announced earlier this week, the advent of a new spy thriller series based on a novel by John le Car. Possibly he was thinking of John Dickson Carré. Also there is a kind of car called le Car. It is no joke being a disembodied voice, waiting for hours to say your line. The same thing happens to one-line walk-ons on stage. 'The carriage will see you now, my lady.' But the average walk-on sometimes gets it right. The average voice-over *never* gets it right.

The first big question posed by Episode One of *Tinker*,

Tailor, Soldier, Spy (BBC2) was: would the series be as dull as its own trailer? Featuring playwright Arthur Hopcraft, who had been charged with the task of adapting the aforementioned John le Car's masterpiece for the small screen, this trailer had been filmed on Hampstead Heath. Hopcraft, bravely sporting the same own-up baldy hairstyle as the present writer, walked in a very ordinary way around the Heath while explaining that any of the other very ordinary people to be seen walking around that same verdant expanse might very well be spies. The camera closed in on people who looked so tremendously ordinary that your suspicions were immediately aroused.

Thus Hopcraft was able to divert suspicion from himself. What better cover, when you think about it, could a KGB master-spy have? Adapting a John le Carré masterpiece for the BBC, you get to meet all the right people. Preparatory articles in the *Radio Times* assured us that Sir Alec Guinness, to whom had fallen the task of impersonating le Carré's hero George Smiley, was granted long interviews with Smiley's original. Presumably Hopcraft was in on that. Thus do the British intelligence chiefs preserve their anonymity, never emerging from the shadows except to meet the playwrights who are going to note down everything they say and the actors who are going to copy everything they do.

In the event, the first instalment of *Tinker, Tailor, Soldier, Spy* fully lived up to the standard set by the original novel. Though not quite as incomprehensible, it was equally turgid. Le Carré's early novels were among the best in the spy genre, but by the time he wrote *TTSS* he had started believing in his own publicity. He shifted the emphasis from plot to character – especially to the character of George Smiley. As the later novels have gone on to prove, Smiley gets less interesting the more interested in him the author gets.

But one should refrain from judgment. Things might pick up. Even in the first episode, there was the fun of trying to distinguish Sir Alec's performance as Smiley from his performances in *The Lavender Hill Mob* and *The Ladykillers*, both of which the BBC screened for purposes of comparison. There was also the fun of listening to some highly stilted dialogue ('Let's talk about Control. Shall we talk about Control, George?') and then finding out from the critics next day that the dialogue had been natural, terse, etc. There was the fun of watching a black, leather-gloved hand parting Venetian blinds. There was so much atmosphere you couldn't find the planet.

In *Public School* (BBC1) the plonking voice of Fran Morrison introduced us to Westminster, which on this showing must be an educational paradise. The teachers all seemed brilliantly qualified to be in charge of their pupils. As for the pupils, they all seemed to combine easy charm with the fanatical motivation of suicide pilots.

I can see no case for abolishing such a school but an excellent case for nationalising it. As Margo McDonald pointed out on a news programme during the week, it makes no sense talking about children going to 'the school of their choice' when choice is something only the well-off can afford.

In *Ring of Bright Water and Beyond* (BBC1) an actor pretending to be Gavin Maxwell went to bed with an otter. Later on in the programme it was established that the same otter bit two finger-tips off one of Maxwell's young male companions, a datum which made you wonder what the furry creature, when it was down there under the blankets, might conceivably have bitten off Maxwell.

16 September, 1979

Joggers

D ESPITE his penchant for spiritual uplift, President Carter has always seemed an improvement on his predecessors, but after last week's jogging triumph you could be excused for wondering.

The BBC news programmes screened some telling lengths of American film devoted to the incident. The President was to be seen lumbering awkwardly along among hundreds of fitter men. The President was then to be seen in close-up, gasping like a tuna who had been on deck for several hours. There was a Secret Service man on each side of him, holding him up. Directional microphones caught what the Secret Service men were saying. 'He's not doing so well.' 'Doesn't seem to be able ... to stand up.'

Here was the final proof that Carter, whatever else he might be, is not bogus. If he had the slightest knack for hokum he would not get into these fixes. He would have started his jog at the back of the field, run a hundred yards very slowly, swerved off the road and started talking to the reporters. He would have made a joke of it, and everybody would have loved him.

But he didn't. He is a jogger by nature. Joggers are people who really believe that they can recapture their youth by taking exercise. The brutal facts suggest that unless you have never lost your youth, and have been taking exercise all the time, then trying to get fit will kill you as surely as a horse-kick to the heart. Open the back door of any squash court in London and the purple-faced corpses of executives come flopping out. Among Fleet Street journalists the death rate from jogging is like the last act of *Hamlet*. Not to accept growing old is the sign of a mis-spent life.

On the other hand, Wilde was certainly right about youth being wasted on the young. Most of us have to reach middle age before we start realising what we could have done with it. Emanating from Manchester, *Something Else* (BBC2) is a new 'open door' programme made by young people for young people, although not-so-young people are cordially invited to tune in. I tuned in, and immediately felt as old as Methuselah, as the hills, as the rocks on which I sat.

The studio was crammed with earnest young people for whom the Beatles were remote historical figures. Punk bands did their numbers, some of which were of real musical vigour, but none of which was any greater challenge to society than a wrecked telephone booth. Everybody present assumed automatically that Radio 1 had kept these bands off the air because of the challenge they offered to society. It seemed far more likely that Radio 1 had kept these bands off the air for the usual reason – i.e., that they sounded interesting.

A young person interviewed a member of the Manchester police force. 'Constable, why do you pick on young people?' It seems probable that young people in Manchester, especially if they are black, stand a good chance of being picked up on suss. Whether these particular interviewing techniques constituted a sound way of getting at the facts remained debatable. A day in the life of an abandoned young mother with two children was filmed in detail. It looked grim. 'The money on the social is no good.' But no questions were asked about how she came to be landed with two children while still a teenager. Presumably society was to blame.

Society is getting easier to blame all the time. *The Labour Party Political Broadcast* (BBC1 and 2) sounded convincing when it pointed out that Tory tax-cuts have benefited the rich, without any indication as yet that the rich plan to benefit the country by investing their gains. Neil Kinnock and Wendy Mantle did the talking. Kinnock is so effective on television that he is bound to be offered a measure of power in the course of time, so it will be instructive to see just how radical he can stay. In the interests of credibility, however, he should do something about his haircut. Take it from a fellow baldy, Neil: no matter how carefully you arrange those strands, the essential you shines through. Own up and you'll feel better. Don't be a jogger.

Panorama (BBC1) had a report on Cambodia, just to show us what politics is like in less favoured parts of the world. There is a case for believing that Cambodia has attained its present condition principally because of machinations on the part of more favoured parts of the world, but none of that detracts from the certainty that Pol Pot ranks high on the list of Great Bastards in History.

There was film of the Khmer Rouge's now happily abandoned torture factory, where the torturers apparently kept a photographic record of everything they got up to, thereby revealing a metaphysical interest in agony which sorted ill with their materialist pretensions. Enough of these photographs were fleetingly on show to make you very glad that you weren't seeing the rest, or the same ones longer.

Being a South East Asian is a tough life. The one thin consolation is that in some parts of the world animals are still treated worse. *Bloody Ivory* (BBC2) showed ivory hunters going about their business. It was immediately apparent that the average elephant is making a great mistake in being so large. If they were really as wise as they are cracked up to be, elephants would be the size of mice and able to run like cheetahs.

Ivory hunters sit around the fire all night toasting poison on to the tips of their arrows. The poison is drained off from a rich puff-adder soup, seasoned with anything else rotten that might be lying around the district. The completed missile is then fired into the elephant. There were suggestions that this takes some skill, but it looked no more difficult than hitting the door of a slowly moving barn.

The elephant takes about six months to die in agony. The highly trained ivory hunters track the animal to the scene of its death throes. Finding a dead elephant in open landscape is doubtless not easy, but you have to remember that these boys have been at it all their lives. The tusks are then hacked out and sent away to be converted into tasteless ornaments. A figure of $50,000 per pair of tusks was mentioned, although it seemed likely that only a proportion of this sum was received by the actual ivory hunters – about enough to buy them a new pair of shorts each.

Despite all the interviewer could do to screw things up, *Frederick Ashton* (BBC2) emerged from his birthday tribute sounding like the great man he is. The questions were fatuous, but his answers were pregnant with a lifetime's experience. Old film of early creations was fascinating, but even more so was new film of Sir Frederick still at work. At seventy-five he still moves like a boy. But then staying supple is his profession, not some idle dream. No jogger he.

23 September, 1979

Black dog

BILLED as being 'from an idea by Cedric Messina', *Churchill and the Generals* (BBC2) was a whopping play by Ian Curteis dealing with Churchill's role as our leader during the Second World War (from an idea by Adolf Hitler).

Also known as 'the BBC's largest-ever single drama production', the play uncoiled its slow length through half the night. It had everything going against it. Actors had to come on, pretend to be someone extremely famous, and go off. To help them create these characters they were given dialogue so peppered with anachronistic words that the sense of the past evaporated every time it formed. With all that said, however, the thing still held your attention. Winnie brought it off.

Chosen for the mighty task of reincarnating our hero, Timothy West was the man responsible for ultimate victory. He started the war facing grave difficulties. He was critically short of proper scenes. Instead he had to make what he could out of a succession of quick exchanges in which actors pretending to be generals pointed at maps. But he won through. Reasonably speakable lines started to arrive in sufficient quantities. Some of these were authentically Churchillian, others were acceptable pastiche. They gave him the tools and he finished the job.

The resulting portrait, though it had large gaps within, was at least rounded. Churchill was shown to be a mean-minded bully as well as a great spirit. He was also shown to have a romantic impracticality by which he frequently sabotaged his own historical sense. His famous 'black dog' depressions were here plausibly shown to be brought on by memories of his First World War Dardanelles disaster, which for some reason he tended to repeat at every opportunity during the Second World War as well, perhaps in the hope of laying the ghost.

Churchill was shown behaving shabbily towards Wavell, a more cultivated and judicious man than he was, although not as charismatic. Churchill was shown being a pain in the neck generally. This was probably already on the limit of what most British people who lived through the war can bear to hear at the present time about the man who they believe – quite rightly, in my view – saved them from tyranny. There is no point carping too hard about what was left out, although a lot was. Area bombing, for example, was not even mentioned.

Churchill thought that a bombing offensive against the German cities was the only way of delaying a second front while still being seen to be making an effort. If his tactical imagination had been as good as he thought it was, he might have found a more effective and less barbaric alternative. As things were, he and Harris – whom he was later careful to repudiate, and who indeed was very hard to find in this play, unless he was one of the extras in blue uniforms – sent a generation of our best young men to a death which history will find it difficult to call honourable, since so many innocent men, women and children were burned in the fires.

But the fires are out, except as memories. By now the whole matter is a war of words. Instead of bombs dropping on German towns, we have Mr Curteis dropping on the English language. I get sick of hearing myself say in this column that there is no point spending thousands of pounds getting sets and costumes in period if the dialogue spends most of its time popping out of it. Everybody in the play said 'massive' to mean 'large' – a most unlikely usage for the 1940s.

Winston Churchill wrote and spoke English floridly, but with some precision. If he meant that things were tense, he would say 'tense', not 'fraught' – a slovenly usage which did not come in for another twenty years at least. Mr Curteis might be able to supply chapter and verse to show that Churchill committed all these solecisms and more, but from my own memories I doubt it.

Three instalments of *Tinker, Tailor, Soldier, Spy* (BBC2) have by now crawled past on their way to oblivion, and even the most dedicated fan must be starting to wonder. The second episode was set mainly in Lisbon and showed a young male spy (one of ours) and a young female something-or-other (one of theirs) engaged in a protracted exchange of cryptic dialogue. Forty minutes of screen-time yielded about forty seconds of exposition. The rest was atmospherics, which included a lady singer yodelling in profile, so that the lighting could bounce artily off her teeth. The boredom was paralysing. What would George Smiley make of all this?

George Smiley made a meal of it, as usual. In the third episode he was hot, or rather lukewarm, on the trail. In Oxford he picked the addled brains of the legendary Connie, queen of the filing cabinets. Connie is one of John le Carré's most inspired creations, since she makes any secretary who buys his books think that there is something really dangerous and romantic about filing. Connie (Beryl Reid) and Smiley (Alex Guinness) wetly kissed each other. It was the heaviest piece of action in the whole episode.

Sir Alec's performance is a triumph. For a man who has scaled all the heights of his profession, and who owns $2\frac{1}{4}$ per cent of *Star Wars* into the bargain, it can't be easy to play a mental defective. The constant temptation must be to go for cheap laughs. Instead, he finds a thousand ways per episode of looking puzzled but determined. He raises his left eyebrow. He purses his lips. He raises his right eyebrow. Now see the infinite subtlety with which he lowers the left eyebrow while keeping the right eyebrow raised. But wait! Isn't there a smile playing on those pursed lips? (Smiling with pursed lips is not easy, but after fifty years in the business Sir Alec is the master of his instrument. He could probably even copy June Allyson's trick of pouting and lisping simultaneously.) Hold it! He's going to say something. 'What's ... going ... *on*?'

What's going on is a concerted attempt to inflate a thin book into a fat series. The third le Carré novel, *The Spy Who Came in from the Cold*, had enough plot for a single film. The same applied to *Call for the Dead*, filmed as *The Deadly Affair*. *TTSS* is bulkier than either of those two books, but has less plot. It might have made two mildly riveting episodes on television. Spread out over a whole series it grips you like a marshmallow. The characters just aren't interesting enough to survive that much exposure. Smiley is Sherlock Holmes with a flighty wife. Somewhere out there over the curve of the world, Karla is imitating Moriarty. Dwell on them and they crumble.

Panorama (BBC1) caught spy fever too. Tom Mangold told us about 'a superpower spy war stretching across two continents'. Apparently a Soviet agent has been found dead in a Swiss bath. A filmed reconstruction showed us a close-up of his hairy knees. These, it seems, have caused 'raised eyebrows across two continents'. Sir Alec Guinness could raise his eyebrows across two continents, but I doubt if anybody else could.

30 September, 1979

Negative, Captain

'WHAT in the name of ... ?' cries Bones in *Star Trek* (BBC1 recurring). The Starship *Enterprise* has been seized by some mysterious force. Even with all engines at Full

Impulse Power the ship is stymied, leaving the Trekkies with nothing to fall back on except their lavish supplies of dot-dot-dot dialogue.

The last episode of *Star Trek* was made years ago, but the series obeys Einstein's laws of space and time, forever circumnavigating the universe on its way back to your living room. By the time each episode returns there has been a red-shift in the dialogue. Astronomers assure us that white light stretches as its source moves away from us, showing up red. *Star Trek* dialogue stretches in direct proportion, yielding the dot-dot-dot effect.

'Am I ... seeing things?' cries the strangely named Chekov. The scanners have revealed that the force squeezing the ship is emanating from a giant, disembodied, green hand. Our attention is thereby momentarily distracted from Chekov's weirdo haircut, which otherwise would take a lot of explaining. In the Wimpy Bar which serves as the starship's bridge, all are alert in the face of imminent destruction. Even Captain Kirk looks tense. 'Is it ... a hand?' he asks. 'Negative, Captain,' murmurs the imperturbable Mr Spock. But even Spock's dialogue is coming out dotted. 'Not a human appendage ... a field of energy.'

Lt Uhura, the starship's sexy black female communications officer, has figured the whole thing out in a flash, but her dialogue is slow to catch up. 'It's almost as if it means ... to grab us!' At this point a shimmering before the viewer's eyes indicates that one of two things is happening. Either the viewer's brain is packing up completely, or else the previous week's episode has caught up with the episode he thought he was watching.

The latter proves to be the case. Spock, Kirk, Scottie and Mr Sulu have suddenly appeared on the surface of a planet that looks exactly like a set. Appropriately enough, the planet seems to be populated exclusively by bad actors.

One of the bad actors is a lovely witch called Sylvia. Taking the form of a giant cat, she drugs Scottie and Sulu.

'They appear to be ... drugged, Jim,' murmurs Spock. But Kirk has noticed something mysterious about that cat. Perhaps he has noticed that it is as big as a horse.

'That cat ... Hmm.' The moggie retransmogrifies itself back into Sylvia, who drapes herself warmly on the broad starboard shoulder of the scrumptious Kirk. 'You ... Why do I find you ... different?' Kirk fights for control as his nostrils fill with the local equivalent of Joy by Patou. Overhead, the *Enterprise* is once again in the grip of 'a force field of some kind'.

Bloop, Bleep, Bawoing. The episode *before* the episode before has started to arrive. At Star Base 11, the *Enterprise* is in dry-dock being treated for atomic piles. Kirk is on trial for cowardice. One of his old girlfriends, who are apparently scattered through the galaxy like cosmic dust, is the prosecuting attorney. Counsel for the defence is Elisha Cook Jr, transferred by time-warp from an old Humphrey Bogart movie. Things look bad for Kirk. But Spock is playing three-dimensional chess against the ship's computer, whose console resembles a collection of dashboards from pre-war Detroit cars. It turns out that the computer is the coward. Spirk has saved Kock! I mean, Spock has saved Kirk! All ahead Warp Factor One!

Something Else (BBC2) continues to make every other youth-slanted show on the air look like something Billy Cotton Jr dreamed up in a luke-warm bath. The latest instalment came from Birmingham. Future programmes will be made in other places, such as Plymouth. Whether Plymouth will prove as rich a source of gritty urban interest as Birmingham remains to be seen, but for the moment it can confidently be said that *Something Else* is actually doing, in its naive way, what so many sophisticated programmes have tried to do but failed. It gives you the feel of city life.

Sometimes the feel is of something unspeakable, as of a dead toad. The punks, especially, are not always easy to love. 'Oi dress this way because oi'm into poonk.' Yes, but why have you got a bolt through your head? A girl who has applied her pink eye-shadow with boxing gloves informs the semi-articulate interviewer that minority groups are always picked on. She has a nose like a pin cushion. 'Obviously if you dress different there's going to be a lot of aggression against you,' says a boy with a green plaid suit, a chalk white face and hair like a carrot going nova.

The Rastafarians were shown at work and play. It was clear that they work hard. The programme is race-relations conscious without being pious about it. Indeed aggro flies freely around the studio at all times. The music and dancing are about fifty times better than anything that happens on the dire *Roadshow Disco* (BBC1). Punk music loosens my fillings, but those who like it presumably want to hear the best bands available and *Something Else* apparently knows which rocks to lift up in order to find them.

What the show needs most is a link-man as original as its content. In the latest episode they have found him. His name is Paul Kenna. He looks about eighteen years old, keeps falling out of cupboards in his pyjamas and talks a stream of surrealist gibberish funny enough to make you hope they'll bring him back.

The first episode of the new arts programme *Mainstream* (BBC2) was a thin-shelled egg laid from high altitude. Originally a brain-child of Tony Palmer's, the programme was apparently intended to function as a nationwide creativity round-up, but somewhere along the road to the studio it had been transformed into a low-budget revue. A link-man introducing Claudio Abbado pronounced his first name Clordio instead of Clowdio, perhaps in order to put provincial listeners at their ease.

The said Clordio was then interviewed by someone billed as Lady Jane Wellesley, whose main line of questioning concerned the maestro's interest in football. In a future programme Lady Jane might care to interview Kevin Keegan about his interest in Scarlatti. Or perhaps Scarlatti could interview Lady Jane about Kevin Keegan. While the details are being worked out, the show could perhaps be brought in for repairs, or, failing that, towed further out to sea and sunk by gunfire.

Panorama (BBC1) featured Jane Fonda in her latest role of responsible political candidate. Other women, Jane assures us, envy her because of her sense of purpose. That is why they are overawed by her when she talks. 'I see this glaze that I am very familiar with.' The same glaze is over my eyes right now, just from thinking about her. 'I'm a consciousness raiser.' She certainly raises my consciousness. If ever I find myself sharing a belief with her, I re-examine it immediately.

Tosca in Tokyo (BBC2) featured Montserrat Caballé. The Japanese were impressed. It was clear that they hadn't seen anything that size since the battleship *Missouri* anchored in Tokyo Bay in 1945.

14 October, 1979

Really terrible

LATEST guest host of *Friday Night ... Saturday Morning* (BBC1) was Sir Harold Wilson, erstwhile Prime Minister of Great Britain. Those of us who expected him to be terrible received a shock. He was *really* terrible.

His guests did their best to help him out, especially Harry Secombe, who was first on. Harry attempted to lighten the atmosphere by saying 'Whee hee hee!' That having failed to produce results, he switched to 'Na-*hah*! Na-hah na-hah na-*hah*!' He then addressed Sir Harold disarmingly as 'Sir Harold Parkinson', to see how that would work. The audience dutifully convulsed itself, a cue for Sir Harold to remind Harry about the longevity of their friendship. 'We've known each other for years.'

Pat Phoenix, Freddie Trueman and somebody calling him-self Tony Benn succeeded Harry in the role of interlocutor. Sir Harold's wit sparkled fitfully as he attempted to make his presence felt, usually when someone else was talking. He read the autocue as if it were the Rosetta Stone arranged on rollers. Interviewing somebody on the air is a cinch as long as you listen to what he says. This however, is not easy to do if you are busy trying to remember what to ask him next. Inter-viewing somebody on the air is consequently not as easy as it usually looks. The great merit of Sir Harold's stint as a chat-show host was that he made it look as tricky as it is.

What had he expected? What arrogance led him to take the job on with so little preparation? Was he as thoughtless and conceited when he was Prime Minister? But it might easily have gone the other way. There is no law which says that a politician can't host a chat show. Shirley Williams is a case in point. Even at its dullest, *Shirley Williams in Conversa-tion* (BBC1) has provided substantial talk. She has established herself immediately as one of the most formidable performers on television, and probably hasn't done her long-term politi-cal prospects much harm either.

Her latest guest was Willy Brandt. In sharp contrast to other quondam premiers who shall remain nameless, Brandt is a man of stature and vision, but for an English-speaking interviewer he is not necessarily easy meat, since his English, although good enough to sound like his first language, is not sufficiently flexible to express his ideas fluently. Mrs Williams did the right thing and gave him time. As a result we heard the rationale of the *Ostpolitik* directly from its inventor's mouth.

Mrs Williams rather overdoes the business of holding her chin thoughtfully. All she has to do now is relax and she'll be ideal. She has so much real personality that there is no necessity for her to do anything but be herself. The first requirement of being yourself, of course, is having a self to be. Were Sir Harold Wilson to relax and be himself, he would either contract suddenly to a small, white, not very hot dot, or else blow himself all over the studio, leaving scraps of limp skin hanging from the gantry.

Chairman Hua of China did a quiet number on the current affairs programme *Newsweek* (BBC2). (The Beeb's executives must save a lot of wear and tear on the brain by calling programmes after magazines. Look forward to programmes called *Encounter*, *National Geographic* and *Proceedings of the Aristotelian Society*.) It was not easy to tell whether Hua was on the up-and-up, since the interview was conducted by Felix Greene, whose access to China has always depended on his willingness to ask only those questions which fit the prepared answers. But since the film he brings back is more interesting than no film at all, *Newsweek* was well justified in running his latest effort. Richard Kershaw came on at the start to excuse 'this departure from our normal style'. By style he meant standards, but there was no need to be ashamed.

After a breathtaking opening sequence, in which Felix Greene arrived at Hua's residence to be informed that the Chairman was expecting him, the intrepid film-maker sat down and got on with the job of nodding gratefully while Hua cranked out the usual quota of agitprop slogans which in Communist countries serve as a substitute for political analysis. Mao, it appears, remains the fountainhead of all wisdom. His wonderful revolution came within a whisker of being hijacked by the Gang of Four. Everything that went wrong after Mao's death was due to 'sabotage by Lin Piao and the Gang of Four'. The task now is to make up 'the time lost through their sabotage'.

There were some action shots of Hua underlining things with a pencil, but he was soon back to castigating the Gang of Four. Six million people had appeared on the streets to demand that the Gang of Four be put on ice. There was no need to add that these six million people had put in their appearance 'spontaneously', but Hua added it anyway, perhaps afraid that Mr Greene would miss the point.

Hua had good grounds for supposing that Mr Greene, if left unprompted, would miss any point in the world, since it apparently never occurred to him to ask the only question that mattered – the one about what was so wise about Mao if he couldn't see the Gang of Four coming, especially when one of them was his wife.

21 October, 1979

Maging a moggery

MAIN business of the week was the showdown between *Kissinger and Frost* (LWT), an edited version of the NBC encounter which in America had caused a certain amount of fuss, since Kissinger had insisted on eking out the question-and-answer with a few prepared speeches. By the time NBC's doctored version reached your screen via LWT, it was looking a bit bitty. Nevertheless it was gripping stuff. Frost nowadays sings instead of talks, but if you could compensate mentally for his fluctuating intonation it gradually became apparent that he had done a certain amount of homework and was willing to put the modern Metternich on the spot if he could.

Kissinger had few vocal devices with which to combat Frost's deadly technique of delivering his questions as fragments of a baritone aria. All Kissinger could do was fall back on his old trick, or drick, of substituting, or subsdiduding, 'd' for 't'. His line on Vietnam was familiar. 'We inherided a dragedy.' This standpoint being not without substance, he was able to defend it with some force.

Indeed Frost's questioning, though admirably implacable, was often wide of the mark. Frost had obviously bought the entire anti-war package on Cambodia, up to and including the idea that the North Vietnamese had scarcely even been present within its borders. They were there all right. There was considerable military justification for US intervention in Cambodia, as even some of the most severe critics of Nixon and Kissinger are prepared to admit. 'Now jusd a minude,' fumed Kissinger. 'With all due respecd, I think your whole line of quesdioning is maging a moggery of whad wend on in Indo-China.'

Well, not quite. Nixon and Kissinger might have had short-term military reasons for their policy on Cambodia, but the ruinous long-term consequences were easily predictable. Nor, despite Kissinger's plausible appeal to international law, was there anything legal about the way he and his President tried to keep the bombing secret. In fact they conspired to undermine the United States Constitution. Kissinger's personal tragedy is that his undoubted hatred of totalitarianism leads him to behave as if democracy is not strong enough to oppose it.

Unfortunately his personal tragedy, when he was in power, transformed itself into the tragedy of whole countries. The most revealing part of the interview was not about South East Asia, but about Chile. It transpires that a 36 per cent share of the popular vote was not enough to satisfy Kissinger that Allende had been democratically elected. Doubtless remembering Hitler, who had got in on a comparable share of the total vote, Kissinger blandly ascribed Allende's electoral victory to a 'peculiaridy of the consdidution'. But Margaret Thatcher is Prime Minister of Great Britain by the same kind of peculiarity, and presumably Kissinger, if he were still ruling the roost, would have no plans to topple her. By what right did he topple Allende?

Kissinger couldn't even conceive of this as a question. 'Manipulading the domesdig affairs of another goundry', he explained, 'is always gombligaded.' It is not just complicated, it is often criminal. The Nixon–Kissinger policy in Chile was an unalloyed disaster, which delivered the population of that country into the hands of torturers and gave Kissinger's totalitarian enemy their biggest propaganda boost of recent times. You didn't have to be Jane Fonda to hate the foreign policy of Nixon and Kissinger. All you had to be was afraid of Communism.

These were general points which, if Frost had borne them firmly in mind, might have led him to ask more searchingly specific questions. He deserves some credit for having tried hard, but finally he was out-matched. Kissinger, for all his faults, is a man of wide culture and real intellect.

Year Zero (ATV) featured John Pilger in Cambodia. Most of what he had to show was hard to look at. Already it has become apparent that Pol Pot's crimes, like Hitler's and Stalin's, are too hideous to take in, even when you are faced with the evidence. Nevertheless Pilger might have found a few unkind things to say about the North Vietnamese, who, I seem to remember, have recently taken to offering their internal enemies the opportunity of going on long yachting expeditions with insufficient regard to safety precautions.

Pilger loudly accused the international relief organisations of playing politics, but forgot to mention the possibility that the North Vietnamese might be playing politics themselves. The way he was telling it, they were philanthropists. He was there and we were here, but it was hard to quell the suspicion that one of the reasons he was there was that North Vietnam likes the way he presents such a neat, easily understandable picture.

Panorama (BBC1) portrayed the Czech Government engaged in the unending totalitarian act of impoverishing its own country by persecuting anybody courageous enough to insist on the objective nature of truth. The defendants were accused of 'subversion of the State on a grand scale' and locked up 'in order to safeguard the dictatorship of the proletariat'. Why does it need so much safeguarding?

4 November, 1979

Mother of Shirley Williams

BAD sight of the Week was on *Nationwide* (BBC1): a keen bishop with a cover-up baldy haircut who smugly defended the Church of England's mad scheme to abandon the Authorised Version and the Book of Common Prayer along with it.

People educated in polytechnics, the worthy divine explained, can't understand such arcane verbal forms as 'Our Father, which art in heaven'. His smile of condescension while he articulated these sentiments was further evidence for the theory, widespread among lay students of the Anglican Church, that no clergyman can nowadays attain high office who has not first given solid and continuous proof that he is ga-ga.

There can be little doubt that the Church's evident intention to commit suicide originates right at the top. With the Archbishop of Canterbury himself evidently hell-bent on extirpating the single greatest repository of poetic truth available to the faithful, there is not much hope of events being influenced by mere reason. All a non-believing but seriously concerned layman can do is point out the obvious, which is that these literary treasures, composed at a time when the English language was so strong that even a committee could write it, will stay current for ever, whereas no current version will stay good for a fortnight.

By now it is clear that the BBC is engaged in a vast conspiracy to make Shirley Williams Prime Minister. Her recent, highly successful chat series was but the first move. The second move, less direct but possibly even more effective, is to screen a lavish, thoughtful and touching drama about her mother's life. The first episode of *Testament of Youth* (BBC1), besides taking Mrs Williams several steps nearer No. 10, was one of the best things I have seen on television for some time.

In fact it was one of the best things I have seen on television since *The Girls of Slender Means*, which was directed by Moira Armstrong. *Testament of Youth* is also directed by Moira Armstrong, and once again her handling of cameras is wonderfully delicate. Hers is the kind of technique that never draws attention to itself, which means that she has no more chance of becoming famous than Tony Palmer has of becoming obscure. But her unobtrusively fluent way of moving the camera from face to face at the right time makes an ordinary story subtle and a subtle one profound.

'Mother of Shirley Williams' having sensibly been rejected as a title, it was decided to give the series the same name as the original book. I have not read it, but soon shall, because Vera Brittain was obviously ideally equipped to tell two great stories at once. One story was about her own education as a liberated young woman. The other story was about how the First World War cut down the generation of young men of whom she aspired to be an equal. In Elaine Morgan's literate adaptation the two lines of narrative form a powerfully sad counterpoint. I imagine that in the book the plangent music is more desolating still.

But in the first episode the harvest had not yet begun. The crop was still ripening: beautiful young men playing decent cricket at good schools, they had untroubled brows, possibly because there was not a thought in their heads. Vera's brother was one of these. The pater was in trade, but school was making a gentleman of the son – a smooth process which Oxford would complete. But what of the daughter? Played by the ebullient Cheryl Campbell, Vera had to fight for her freedom all the way against a dumb-cluck mother and a father fond of saying things like 'Stoof and nonsense!'

In fact Mr Brittain was a bit of a Michael Palin character. 'Arm waiting,' he announced, 'to ear what were the meaning of *thut* little exhibition.' Meanwhile brainless Mrs Brittain, a clear case of auto-lobotomy, was panic-stricken lest her daughter's inexplicable desire for education 'spoil her chances'. Some of this came out like parody, but it is hard to see how it could not, since we have forgotten how true it used to be.

Far from regarding the male sex as dominant, I have always thought of it, in comparison to the female one, as bloodless, furtive and lacking in moral fibre. But as the week wore on the television set fell further and further prey to the delusion that the towering stature of womanhood was something I needed to be convinced of. Vera Brittain said her piece and sank back into the shadows, only to be succeeded by Dame Margot Fonteyn. In the first instalment of her big-budget new series *The Magic of Dance* (BBC2) she stood revealed, feet turned elegantly out, as a natural pitch-person. The sheer joy of watching her walk about would have compensated for any verbal deficiencies, but in fact she talks a treat.

Of the performing arts, ballet is the one I have come to last, having been stupidly puritanical about it until recent years. But now I am sorry that I ever stayed away. There is a possibility, however, that my attitude is all wrong. In her excellent book *After-Images*, the American ballet critic Arlene Croce explains that the whole idea of ballet is to transcend sex and that any man who is aroused by looking at a ballerina is missing the point. I am afraid I have been missing the point in a big way, and that when I look at Dame Margot I go on missing it. She is an attractive woman and that's that.

Only in her script did she leave anything to be desired. It ranged back and forth over space and time. Plainly it will go on doing so in future episodes. But there are penalties to be paid for not following a particular subject through while you are focused on it. Fred Astaire, for example, was a perfect object for her attention, but either no film clips were available or else someone had decided not to linger. A montage and an interview were all we got. Perhaps there will be a follow-up in a later episode, but what was required at the time, once the subject had been broached, was at least one dance from Fred and Ginger.

No complaints, though, about the ballet excerpts, which were lavish. Makarova's arms in the *Swan Lake pas de deux* went halfway across the stage on each side. Seymour danced her final scene from *The Sleeping Beauty* with characteristic drama. A ballerina from the Dance Theatre of Harlem moved with such transcendental beauty that I started thinking Arlene Croce might be right after all. Nureyev, whom Dame Margot interviewed at length, was the lad who opened ballet up for the male stars. One is glad about this, but finally it is the ballerinas who are the *fons et origo* of the art.

11 November, 1979

Miss World and Mrs Mao

INDUSTRIAL action, the British name for industrial inaction, tore great holes in *Miss World 1979* (BBC1), but the surviving fragments should have been enough to convince the 300 million frustrated potential viewers that they had come within a whisker of viewing a masterpiece.

Seventy contestants paraded in national dress while a production number of riveting fatuity occurred nearby. The song which inspired the dancers to their gyrations had to do with the qualities that the eventual winner of the 'Miss World' title would evince. 'She may be tall or even small, oh yeah.' It was also predicted that she would have 'that special glow', a contention which suggested that in a lean year the crown might possibly be won by a decaying mackerel.

Sacha Distel then came on. Either his smile had been sutured into position or else he wanted to sing. He wanted to sing. Meanwhile the national dresses were still going past, most of them looking like floats in a procession. One of the South American girls was the point of origin for a towering wicker-work structure covered with feathers. She upstaged all the other contestants by the simple expedient of rendering them invisible. Another girl had a collection of flags growing out of her back.

They all went off to be cut out of their national dress with acetylene torches and axes. Time for Sacha to be joined by Esther Rantzen. Esther managed to mention her pregnancy in her first sentence. Everybody in Britain already knew, but among the remaining 250 million people scattered all around the world there might have been several who were still in ignorance. Either Sacha was one of these or else he was busy trying to remember his next line, since he did not react. Esther and Sacha then fell to delivering a cross-talk act so deadly that they could not have done worse if they had written it themselves.

Back came the girls in evening dress. Miss Austria was a honey. Miss Spain nearly killed herself falling down the stairs. Somewhere about here the pictures gave out, leaving us with nothing except the head and shoulders of the Beeb's new number one link-man for non-events, Ray Moore. I have tried hard to appreciate Ray's qualities but I keep failing, possibly because he has a way with words that leaves you wondering whether the human race is not perhaps fated to lose the power of speech altogether. 'We've got a little surprise for you,' said Ray, and on came Ronnie Barker's least inspired creation, a dreary little movie called *Futtock's End*.

Who does the BBC think we are? If we have to miss a chunk of the show then we have to miss a chunk of the show. We didn't need a lolly to suck. I had to switch over to *News at Ten* (ITN) to find out what the strike had been caused by. Apparently forty sound technicians had walked off in a huff. Perhaps they had not been allowed to appear in national dress. Why Ray Moore could not have been instructed simply to give us a few facts is a mystery. 'It's a marvellous picture, isn't it?' asked Ray when the movie was over. It wasn't, but the picture of Miss Bermuda was. She had won. On top of that, she was decidedly pretty.

Beauty contests are very silly but then so are brain contests. *Mastermind* (BBC1) gets battier all the time. In the latest instalment a man took agriculture as his special subject. Yes, all of agriculture, any time, anywhere. He did not do well. A woman, on the other hand, took the Dragon Books of Anne McCaffrey. Not surprisingly she did very well indeed. When I go on *Mastermind* I shall elect as my special subject the Throth Books of Wilbur Plartz. Magnus Magnusson will ask such questions as 'Why did the Elf Barf return to the Kingdom of Schnurk?' I will know all the answers.

Someone else who knew all the answers was the second Mrs Mao. She got frequent mentions in *The Arts of Chinese Communism* (BBC2), a highly informative documentary fronted by the Beeb's excellent China hand, Philip Short. It seems that the arts in China are now being allowed to recover from the damage done to them by the Cultural Revolution in general and the vengeful puritanism of the Mk II Mrs Mao in particular. She was obviously an even bigger bitch than we thought.

Ballet is getting back on its points again, but all too slowly. The lady now running the resurgent ballet school spent most of the Cultural Revolution tilling the fields. The high spot of her re-education was looking after pigs, since at least the pigs did not deliver vituperative lectures about bourgeois decadence. Mrs Mao did, and even gave instructions on the correct positions for dancers' feet. Like all cultural commissars, she was an artist manqué.

The Peking Opera is also on its way back, but many of the performers are missing, having been persecuted to death during the period when Mrs Mao was supervising the destruction of traditional forms in favour of truly revolutionary works whose ideological purity was proved by the fact that tickets for them could not be given away with free rice.

18 November, 1979

Out to lernch

STRIKE-STRICKEN on Monday evening, *Nationwide* (BBC1) was replaced by a thrilling programme about growing leeks in the North. Now that the series of strikes is temporarily over we will just have to try getting used to the rare experience of normal conditions.

More fascinating than ever in its current series, *Dallas* (BBC1) continues to offer its uniquely Texan combination of wealth, family conflict and sumptuous, scantily draped females. The men wear Astroturf haircuts topped off with ten-gallon hats. Marginally more *simpatico* this time, J. R. Ewing has a new haircut which changes colour from shot to shot and a hat-band composed of what appear to be crushed budgerigars. In the normal course of events he is an easy man to loathe, but lately he is having a prarlm with his wife. A prarlm is something difficult to solve.

Sue Ellen has had a baby, of which J.R., all unbeknownst to him, is not the father. She used to have a drinkin' prarlm, but quit. Now she has a different prarlm: she hates J.R. 'If we trah, really trah,' J.R. tells her, his hair changing colour and his hat-band fluttering in the wind, 'we can solve all our prarlms.' Sue Ellen sneers at him and doffs her robe preparatory to a dip in the pool. J.R. eyeballs her fair form and declares himself lustful, as well he might, because Sue Ellen is beautiful enough to make a man break down and crah.

Spurned by Sue Ellen, J.R. climbs into his powerful convertible and drives off to lernch. A meal taken in the middle of the day, lernch is when characters in *Dallas* get together to discuss the plot. It transpires that Sue Ellen's baby may well be suffering from neuro-fibrowhosis, a rare disease which attacks children who have been written into a long-running series and may have to be written out again later. Sue Ellen, it is agreed, must not be told. 'Sue Ellen's already so guilty about the baby this could put her over the edge. Don't you understand she's *not well emotionally*?'

Not well emotionally, Sue Ellen climbs languidly out of the pool. She looks quite well in other respects. Beads of chlorinated water cling to her peachy epidermis. But just when you are thinking that no woman could have a more attractively lopsided contemplative smile than Sue Ellen, her sister Kristin comes back. Kristin has been away. That is why she has come back. In order to come back, she had to go away in the first place. Kristin wants J.R. She and Sue Ellen engage in a lopsided contemplative smile competition.

The third beautiful woman in the cast is the level-headed even though lovely Pamela. For a cattle man who's had a hard day at the computer terminal, coming home to discover one or more of these ladies lying around the pool sure takes a weight off his mind. Removing his hat would take even more weight off his mind, but there are limits.

Dallas would have the same basic selling proposition as *Charlie's Angels* – three gorgeous females who partly disrobe one at a time – if it were not for the additional presence of such weirdo supernumeraries as Lucy, a neckless blonde sex grenade only half as high as everybody else. Miraculously preserved, the elder Ewings hover worriedly in the background. Called Jock and Miss Ellie, they are out of an up-market version of *The Waltons*. In fact *Dallas* is like every American soap opera you have ever seen, all rolled into one and given an unlimited charge account at Neiman-Marcus.

Straining to fill its schedules, commercial television is the underdog at the moment, so perhaps it is worth pointing out that the *South Bank Show* (LWT) is one programme, at least, which consistently leaves its BBC equivalent looking pale. Since its BBC equivalent at the moment is the ill-starred *Mainstream* (BBC1) this might not seem much of a compliment, but there is no gainsaying that ITV's big-budget flagship arts round-up justifies its air-time. People who attack the show as cultural dilution can't think much of culture, if they think it can be diluted so easily.

Nobody's reputation gets attacked on the *South Bank Show*. On the other hand nobody's reputation gets enhanced. What happens is usually a wrap-up, rather along the lines of a *Vogue* profile. But a *Vogue* profile can have its uses, especially as an introduction. Germaine Greer was given an episode to expound her thesis about women painters, using as examples the star graduates of the Slade School in the 1890s. Brilliantly refuting her own argument, she inadvertently stumbled on the real reason why so few women painters have been geniuses like Gwen John. According to Dr Greer, men painters make women painters neurotic. But the case of Gwen John suggested that only the rare woman is neurotic enough.

Dr Greer narrated the programme in the characteristically vivid style which her book lacks. The programme was consequently an unexpected bonus to her years of scholarly effort in this subject. In another episode, Glenys Roberts (one of the best practitioners in London of the above-mentioned despised genre, the profile) ably interviewed François Truffaut. It can easily be said that Truffaut scarcely needs introduction, but on the whole Melvyn Bragg is right to assume that it is not just good box office but good sense to go on wheeling out the established names. Besides, those with inflated reputations can be relied on to attack themselves. Talking amiable drivel about Gary Gilmore, Norman Mailer scarcely needed close questioning. All Melvyn had to do was sit there, which he did.

Joyce Grenfell's death gave pause for thought to all who knew her. Between them, she and C. A. Lejeune laid the foundations for this kind of column. When I first came to this country I flattered myself that she took a special interest in my early attempts at writing. Later on I learned that there were scores of us, all thinking of her as our guardian angel. Elegant in all things, she was a great one for economical composition. Her songs and sketches went exactly the right distance and then stopped. She would have had no quarrel with her maker if he felt the same way about her life. Her faith was profound. So was her humour, which was so devoid of malice that some people called her sentimental. She wasn't. She was just greatly good.

9 December, 1979